The General Care & Maintenance of Garter Snakes & Water Snakes

David Perlowin

Table of Contents

Introduction

Garter snakes, ribbon snakes, and water snakes are among the most popular, widely available, attractive and interesting reptile pets. Because most of these species are relatively common, inexpensive, and easy to maintain, they are also among the first reptiles owned by children and budding herpetoculturists. Unlike many of the snakes sold in the pet trade, most garter snakes and water snakes will feed primarily on fish (a diet that can be purchased at the local market), rather than rodents. Add to this the fact that most of these snakes are very docile and easy to handle, and the reasons for their popularity become obvious.

Because these snakes are generally affordable, they are often purchased by impulse buyers who are not prepared to spend the money required to provide the necessary accomodations for the welfare of the animals in captivity. In the minds of many people, cheap pets are often associated with inexpensive captive environments. Many people mistakenly believe that the cost of a setup should in some way be correlated with, and to a degree can be justified by, the cost of the animal. The fact is that keeping reptiles has a cost-of-vivarium-to-cost-of-animal ratio that is generally comparable to keeping tropical fish.

Even though the great majority of the garter snakes and water snakes sold in the pet trade are wild-collected, in recent years there has been an increased interest in the ornamental and commercial potential of these animals. Herpetoculturists are now breeding rare color morphs, including albino lines of various species. More attention has also been given to unusual morphs and variations among wild-collected animals. As a result, the prices of some of the varieties of garter snakes and water snakes sold in the herpetocultural trade are comparable to prices of the more expensive colubrids, such as some of the kingsnakes. New color and pattern morphs, along with commercial products developed to facilitate the care of these species in captivity, should make them even more popular in the future than they are now.

This book is intended to inform beginning and experienced hobbyists about selection, proper housing, feeding, general maintenance and breeding of these snakes. It includes a number of photographs representing several of the species, as well as some of the unusual morphs that are maintained and bred by specialized herpetoculturists.

Before buying a snake

Parents might ask why their child is not only interested in snakes, but also wants to keep one as a pet. The initial reaction is one of alarm because of unfounded fears, lack of concrete information and the belief that other people's children aren't interested in snakes. However, if the child is allowed to have a pet snake, the parents usually become interested as well. Indeed, it is almost essential that they do so for the welfare of the animal. If the child is left to his or her own devices, the snake often will be neglected and a negative experience will result. Thus, for parents it becomes a matter of deciding whether they are committed to keeping the snake healthy and participating with the child in the animal's day-to-day upkeep. This decision is probably the most important one when considering keeping snakes in captivity.

Before buying a garter or water snake, realize that a properly designed vivarium will cost several times the cost of the snake. The snake will also have to be fed a live food diet (goldfish or other fish with the species covered in this book) or will require some kind of food preparation. Common garter snakes *(Thamnophis sirtalis)* are ideal beginners' snakes because of their small size, docility and relative ease of care.

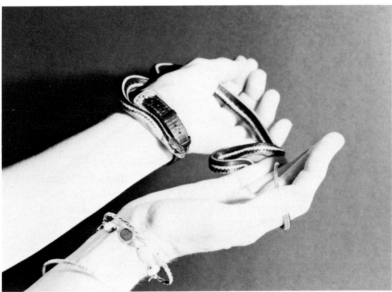

Several members of the genus *Thamnophis,* particularly common garter snakes *(Thamnophis sirtalis),* tend to be very docile. A standard procedure is to allow a snake to move from hand to hand when it is active.

General Information

Classification

Classification is the means by which scientists have categorized plants and animals that live or have lived on Earth. The present system of classification is largely based upon the work of Linnæus, who devised the system of "binomial nomenclature." This system gives each plant and animal at least two names. At the time the system was implemented, Latin was more or less the international language. Thus, almost all scientific classification is in Latin, with some Greek also being used. The first name given is the "genus," which is always capitalized; the second is that of the "species," which is always lower case. In addition, there is the possibility of a third name, the "subspecies," also always lower case.

Further classification is arranged in ascending order of generalities. This system is as follows: genus (plural, genera), family, order, and class. To classify the snakes being discussed in this book, refer to the following table.

Garter snake, ribbon snake, and water snake classification:

Genera:	*Thamnophis, Nerodia, Natrix, Amphisema, etc.*
	Garter, ribbon, and water snakes, etc.
Subfamily:	Natricinae
	Water snakes and allies
Family:	Colubridae
	Typical Snakes
Suborder:	Serpentes
	All Snakes
Order:	Squamata
	Lizards and Snakes
Class:	Reptilia
	All Reptiles

The family Colubridae or "typical snakes" includes kingsnakes, milk snakes, and rat snakes, to name a few, and represents one of the most popular groups of snakes kept in captivity. It is the largest family of snakes, with approximately 250 genera and over 2500 species. Some of the larger colubrids are among the easiest snakes to keep and breed.

The natricines, including garter snakes and water snakes, are non-constricting species that overpower prey primarily by sheer jaw strength. Consequently, they are usually limited to feeding on relatively small prey species (except for dead prey) when compared with constrictors, such as some of the boids. Most natricines feed on fish and amphibians while others, particularly smaller species, will feed on earthworms and other invertebrate prey. Some species such as the queen snake *(Regina septemvittata)* are crayfish specialists (see Rossi 1992 for the care of some of these specialized species). This book focusses on the garter and ribbon snakes of the genus *Thamnophis* (19-20 species) and North American water snakes of the genus *Nerodia* (9 species).

All of the American natricines are live-bearing while most of the Eurasian species lay eggs.

Some of the Asian and Australian species are venomous *(Enhydris, Rhabdophis)*, so correct identification of snakes from these areas is important.

Before collecting . . .
Always check federal and state laws. The San Francisco garter snake is protected under the Endangered Species Act. Several states also protect or have laws regulating collection of garter snakes.

Distribution
All the snakes covered in this book are members of the Natricinae, a subfamily of the family Colubridae. The natricines are primarily semi-aquatic-to-aquatic snakes, largely confined to North America, Eurasia and tropical Asia (Zug 1993). There are no natricines in South America and only a small number of species in Africa and Australia. For the most part, garter, ribbon, and water snakes of the genera *Thamnophis* and *Nerodia* range from southern Canada south to Honduras in Central America, with the bulk of the species found in the United States (not including Alaska and Hawaii).

Longevity
When compared to some of the more popular colubrids and boids, natricine snakes are relatively short lived, although most captivity records are based on animals initially collected as adults from the wild. As a general rule, it would be reasonable to state that most natricine snakes sold in the pet trade have a potential longevity of three to six years for ribbon snakes and five to twelve years for most garter snakes and water snakes. There is a record of a blotched water snake *(Nerodia erythrogaster transversa)* living 14 years and 9 months in captivity (from a juvenile) and of a midland water snake *(Nerodia sipedon pleuralis)* living 9 years and 7 months (from an adult). There are also records of a Northwestern garter snake

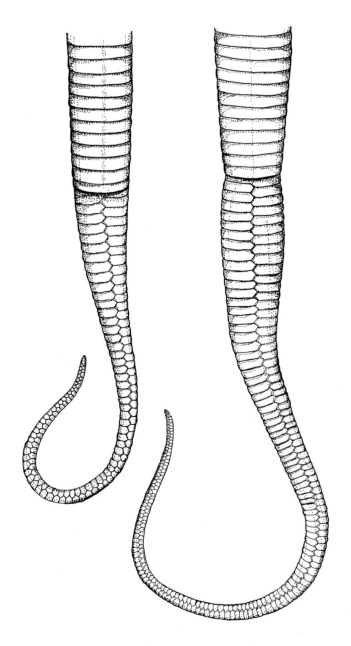

Ventral view of vents and tails of female (left) and male (right) garter snakes. Note the more extreme taper of the tail of the female and the thicker appearance of that of the male. Illustration by Margaret Hawley.

(Thamnophis ordinoides) living 15 years and 11 months as an adult, of a coast garter snake *(Thamnophis elegans terrestris)* living 12 years and 8 months (from a juvenile) and of an eastern garter snake *(Thamnophis sirtalis sirtalis)* living 10 years in captivity. All above records are from Slavens (1992).

Sexing

It can be difficult to determine the sex of most genera of snakes by sight, because the sex organs are internal and there are no obvious physical differences between the sexes. As a general rule, female natricines tend to be larger and more heavy-bodied than males. Males are typically more slender and have paired sex organs called hemipenes, which are housed in the tail, starting at the cloaca. As they become sexually mature, the presence of the hemipenes and additional muscle mass in the tail area of male snakes will noticeably affect their appearance. Thus, with groups of mature garter snakes or water snakes, sex can be determined with some reliability by comparing the tails of various animals. The tails of males will taper more gradually and will generally appear thicker than the tails of females. All things being equal, the tails of males will also tend to be longer than those of females.

Both immature and adult garter snakes and water snakes can also be sexed with a high degree of reliability with the use of a sexing probe. This involves one person holding an animal while another gently pulls back the anal scale and inserts a sexing probe into one of two openings in the sides of the cloaca leading to an inverted hemipenis in males, or to a hemipenis homologue in females. The probe will typically penetrate significantly deeper into a male hemipenis than into the female hemipenis homologue. This procedure can be performed either by knowledgeable personnel at a reptile specialty shop or by an experienced veterinarian.

Skin and shedding

The skin of all snakes is very elastic, which is one of many adaptations which allows for the swallowing of large prey. Consisting of three layers, the outermost epidermal layer forms the distinctive overlapping scales present everywhere on the body. The scales are made of keratin, the same material human nails are made of, and can be smooth or rough. All American garter snakes and water snakes have rough scales, textured with distinctive keels down their centers. The scales on the belly are large, uniform and overlapping, with a special scale covering the cloaca or anal opening. This anal scale is either single, as in all garter snakes, or divided in two, as in all water snakes.

At periodic intervals, a snake must shed its outermost layer of skin. The term for this process is "ecdysis," which is accomplished by the snake secreting a substance between the middle and outer layers of skin, which gives the snake a dull, milky look all over its body, including its eyes. This lasts for several days, until the secretion is absorbed by the skin; the snake then loses the milky look and is ready to shed. It begins by rubbing its snout against the most convenient rough place available, such as a rock or branch. All snakes have no eyelids, but the eyes are covered by a single clear scale which must be shed during ecdysis. During normal ecdysis the skin is shed in one piece, winding up inside out as the snake moves. As a general rule, younger, more rapidly-growing snakes will shed at one month intervals, while adult animals will shed every two to four months.

A summary of the functions of ecdysis is as follows: Snakes shed to accommodate growth, when the skin needs repair, and at various stages of the reproductive cycle (i.e., a few weeks out of hibernation and a few days before laying eggs or giving birth). Additional functions include the generation of a skin scent (including pheromones) during the breeding cycle and the protective or cryptic advantage of the pattern and color of new skin.

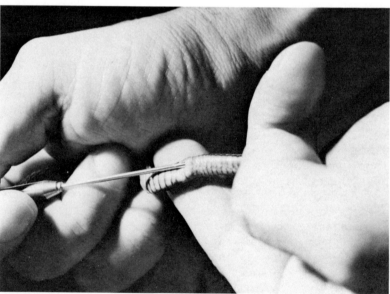

Determining the sex of a garter snake with the use of a sexing probe. Experience and a certain gentle finesse are required to properly perform this procedure.

Selecting a Potentially Healthy Garter Snake, Ribbon Snake, or Water Snake

The vast majority of these species sold in the pet trade are wild-caught adults or captive-born (not captive-bred) babies. Only albino color phases are captive-bred (on a small scale) commercially in the United States on a regular basis. Because wild-caught animals can be difficult to handle and/or may have health problems that could require veterinary care, taking the time to select a potentially healthy animal becomes very important. The following guidelines will help you with the selection process.

1. Before handling the animal you are interested in buying, visually inspect it. Check overall body shape to be certain backbone and/or rib outlines are not prominent. Make sure there are no depressions on the sides of the body indicating broken ribs. Check the skin for sores or scabs which might indicate rough handling or a snake kept in poor conditions. While still in its cage, look for "gaping" or troubled breathing which might indicate a respiratory or parasite problem.

2. The next step is to have the snake handed to you. Since you will more than likely be dealing with a wild-caught adult animal, this may present problems. The snake may exhibit unpleasant behaviors, such as musking and biting. It might be worthwhile to initially handle the snake with gloves on until it calms down. Eventually, the snake can be handled and muscle tone can be checked. A healthy animal should feel strong and give an impression of vigor. Snakes that appear lethargic or limp are very likely in poor health and should not be considered for purchase.

3. Even if the snake has passed the first two steps, further inspection is still necessary, starting with the head. Have someone assist in holding the snake's body while you hold it behind the head. With your free hand, pull down on the lower lip to examine the gum and tooth line. Both sides should be inspected. Look for the presence of bubbly mucus in the mouth, which indicates the possibility of a respiratory infection. Red spots along the jawline may be a sign of the initial stages of stomatitis (mouthrot) and a caseous (cheesy-looking) matter indicates advanced stomatitis. Avoid purchasing animals with any of these symptoms.

4. While still holding the head, check the eyes to be sure they are clear with no cloudiness, scar tissue, or injuries. You may want to postpone your examination of any snake found to be in shed.

5. Release the head of the snake and let it move between your hands. Using your fingertips, feel for indentations or lumps along the length of the body. Snakes with these symptoms should not be purchased.

6. Check the skin of the snake for scars or injuries. Check the ventral (belly) scales for stained, damaged, or raised scales. These indicate the likelihood that the snake was kept on a damp substrate and now has scale rot, a bacterial disease that will require treatment. Animals with these symptoms should be avoided.

7. Mites are usually not a problem with garter, ribbon, and water snakes, but improper maintenance procedures over time could lead to an infestation. Look for tiny beadlike insects crawling on the skin of the snake or on your hands after handling the snake. Also, look for tiny white specks (mite feces) scattered over the body of the snake. Inspect the rim of the eye, which is a favorite place for mites to hide. A raised eye rim is a reliable indication of the presence of mites. Mites can be <u>very</u> difficult to eradicate and they can spread throughout your reptile collection. Unless you must have a particular specimen, avoid a mite-infested snake.

8. Inspect around the opening of the cloaca (vent). The scale covering the cloaca should lie flat and be undamaged and unstained. Check for smeared fecal material near the surrounding area. Avoid snakes with these symptoms.

9. After inspection, practice good personal hygiene; wash your hands throroughly with a bacteriocidal soap. Some snake diseases can be contracted by humans.

Selection of a healthy garter snake will require handling and close inspection.

Acclimation of Wild-Caught Snakes

A significant percentage of wild-caught garter, ribbon, and water snakes acclimate well to captive conditions, although there are many exceptions. On the other hand, the great majority of captive-bred snakes adapt very well to captivity and are willing feeders. The following procedures will greatly improve the chances of wild-caught snakes adapting well to captivity.

1. A cage should be prepared in advance of the snake's arrival home (see Housing section), preferably in a quarantine area away from the rest of your collection. If you are keeping other reptiles, quarantine reduces the risk of the new snake transmitting any disease it may carry. Newspaper is the best ground medium for easy monitoring and cleanup during this period. A shelter (there are several types available commercially) and a large water bowl should be provided. Materials and tools used for cleaning and maintenance should be used on only one cage. If tools are to be used on another setup, they should be disinfected with a 5% bleach solution prior to reuse. The quarantine period should last 8 to 12 weeks, depending on the apparent health of the animal(s). Personal hygiene is _very_ important while dealing with quarantined animals. Use disposable latex gloves (available at most pharmacies); wash your hands with a bacteriocidal soap, such as Betadyne® scrub. As a matter of course, maintenance of quarantine animals should occur _after_ maintenance of your established collection in order to reduce the risks of spreading disease organisms.

2. Wild-collected snakes sold in the pet trade may harbor life-threatening (to the snake) levels of internal parasites and it is highly recommended that you have a stool sample analyzed by a qualified veterinarian. Snakes collected from the wild (rather than purchased through pet stores), which have been spared the overcrowded disease-spreading conditions found in the housing conditions of most pet distributors, are less likely to harbor life-threatening levels of internal parasites and bacterial infections. Because the cost of a fecal exam and parasite treatment may be several times the cost of garter snakes and water snakes, most herpetoculturists (particularly beginners) use a wait-and-see approach before resorting to a veterinary consultation. If a snake feeds well, maintains and eventually gains weight and has formed feces rather than runny feces, then it is considered to be healthy and acclimating. If a snake feeds but loses weight and has watery or unusually smelly feces, then it is considered to require parasite

treatment. This works well as long as you have impeccable maintenance procedures that would prevent the spread of disease in your collection. One approach used by many herpetoculturists is to routinely treat all natricines for nematode roundworms with Panacur® (fenbendazole) and for flagellate protozoans with Flagyl® (metronidazole). Veterinarians who have a broad knowledge of some of the problems with wild-collected reptiles can help you obtain the medication and establish a treatment regimen for natricines. For more information on parasite treatment, see Klingenberg (1993) or Frye (1991).

3. Initially, leave the animal alone after you've brought it home. Do not handle it during the quarantine period, except during weighing, examination, parasite treatment, etc., or to transfer it to another container to allow for cage cleaning.

4. After the initial period of acclimation and parasite treatment, start normal feeding procedures (see Feeding section).

A plastic storage box/shelf system designed by Sandmar (El Cajon, California). These systems allow for housing large numbers of snakes in simple, easily maintained enclosures, while providing segregation that will limit the spread of disease.

Housing

Types Of Enclosures

There are several types of enclosures that can be used to house garter, ribbon and water snakes. Because the appropriate size of the enclosure is dependent upon the size of the snake(s) being kept and because the sizes of individuals in this group of snakes vary from 1 1/2 to 5 feet, a general formula will have to be used. It has been suggested that not only size, but the activity level of snakes also be considered when choosing the proper-size vivarium. Thus, it is recommended that the minimum enclosure size (L x W x H) be 2/3 to 1 1/2 times the length (L) of the snake x 1/3 the length of the snake for the width (W) x 1/3 to 1/2 the length of the snake for the height (H). With more than one snake, at least one foot should be added to the length of the enclosure for each additional animal. This means that for most garter snakes and water snakes, commercially sold vivaria 24 in. (10 gallons) to 36 in. long (30 to 40 gallons) will be adequate for maintaining single adult specimens.

By far the most easily obtained and perhaps best enclosures are the all-glass vivaria with screen tops that are now found in most pet stores. They allow for good visibility, easy cleaning and ventilation, and are offered in a variety of sizes for either simple or naturalistic vivarium design. The screen top is integrated into the molding around the top; this allows for easy locking. A pin-type locking mechanism prevents escape (a <u>very</u> important feature). Captive snakes <u>must</u> be kept securely, not only for your sake, but for theirs as well.

The second most common enclosure is one made of wood (or melamine-coated wood), with a glass or plexiglass door, with or without screened area(s) for ventilation. This type can be built inexpensively by someone handy with tools. The advantages of these enclosures are that they are easily stackable and have the ability to integrate heating, lighting and water areas into the initial design. Since standing water occupies a significant part of the vivarium, waterproofing the wood with nontoxic materials is recommended for the longevity of the enclosure. Spar varnish is a good waterproofing agent. With melamine-coated wood, the corners should be sealed using clear silicone sealer. When wood caging is used, a separate water container should be provided, regardless of how well the wood is treated. Make sure the design allows easy access for feeding and cleaning and that space is allowed for subtank heating and installation of a heat lamp. A plexiglass partition can be included inside the cage, which will allow segregation of animals when feeding. A section of plexiglass the width of the enclosure can be installed by using non-toxic caulk to attach it to the sides. An access hole should be cut into the plexiglass (before it is installed) to allow free movement from one side of the cage to the other. Melamine-coated wood enclosures with sliding-glass fronts and both lighting and thermostatically controlled heating systems are now sold commercially by companies such as Sandmar of El Cajon, California.

Recently, companies such as Third Wave Vivaria, Inc., (Boca Raton, Florida) have made available all-glass vivaria with sliding-glass fronts, enclosures that can hold up to 4 inches of water. Although somewhat expensive, these front-opening vivaria are outstanding for naturalistic vivarium displays.

Another type of enclosure used successfully for commercial scale housing of the smaller species of *Thamnophis* and *Nerodia* are the clear polyethylene storage boxes and the semitranslucent polystyrene storage boxes available in stores selling housewares. These come in several different sizes and can be used for utilitarian setups and maintenance of large colonies. The three sizes most commonly used (L x W x H) are shoe box (12 x 7 x 3.5 in.), small sweater box (15 x 9 x 5 in.), and large sweater box (20 x 15 x 5 in.). Multiple holes need to be drilled into the top and sides to allow for adequate air flow and to allow moisture to evaporate. The size of the ventilation holes depends upon the size of the snake(s) being housed. Hatchling garter and ribbon snakes can be quite small and will crawl through any hole they can fit through. Commercially sold, clear plastic terraria now available in most pet stores are unsuitable for adult animals; however, they are quite useful when rearing newborns.

A shoe box or large plastic terrarium will be adequate housing for one to three hatchling snakes, depending on the size of the snake(s). A small plastic storage box (sweater box) will be adequate for 1 to 2 sub-adult snakes and large plastic storage boxes can be used to house 1 to 2 adult garter and ribbon snakes. Adults of the smaller species of water snake can be housed and even bred in the larger storage boxes. Plastic storage boxes are not recommended for adults of the larger species of water snakes (those exceeding 36 in.). In high relative humidity areas, plastic storage boxes will generally prove problematical for these snakes unless one can replace part of the top with a screen section. Under high humidity conditions, the inside of storage containers may be constantly wet and lead to the

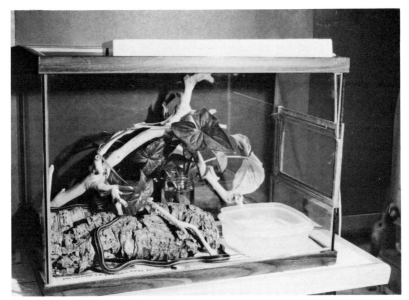

A basic vivarium for housing a pair of garter snakes.

An example of a well-designed vivarium for garter snakes and water snakes, which should include substrate, shelter, large water bowl, climbing/basking area, live plants grown in a jar/container of water, screen top, incandescent bulb in reflector-type fixture, full-spectrum fluorescent lighting and a subtank heater on a rheostat or thermostat. Illustration by Margaret Hawley.

development of diseases, including skin infections. In addition, these storage boxes do not allow enough light for most of these species. This can be remedied by replacing part of the lid with a section of screen and providing full-spectrum fluorescent lighting.

To prevent escape, most commercial colubrid breeders place storage box enclosures on custom-built racks designed so that when an enclosure is inserted between two shelves, the fit is so close that the lid of the storage box cannot be lifted up. The shelves have one side of their upper surface heated with a rheostat controlled heat cable sunk into a routed groove. When placed on a shelf, one section of the storage box will be heated while the other will remain cooler , thereby providing a desirable and easily controlled heat gradient.

Substrate Material
There are several different types of material that can be used on the floor of a vivarium. Newspaper, newsprint or brown paper (recommended during quarantine) are perhaps the easiest types of substrate to change when soiled; they are also the least attractive. A mixture of 50% all-purpose sand (not silica sand) or decomposed granite with 50% peat moss is also quite effective, and more attractive than newspaper. Another effective and attractive substrate is a medium grade orchid bark (fir bark chips) which can be obtained at a plant nursery or pet store specializing in reptiles. This lasts for a relatively long time and is easily changed. Also, some snake keepers use medium grade pea gravel with good success. For those of you who want to set up a naturalistic vivarium planted with sturdy plants, a bottom layer of coarse pebbles covered with a layer of potting soil (free of perlite) is best. A layer of orchid bark can be placed on top and then removed and replaced as it becomes soiled. Remember: In keeping most terrestrial snakes, the surface of the substrate in an enclosure must remain dry. This is particularly important with garter snakes and water snakes.

Enclosure Design/Landscaping
There are certain minimum requirements when furnishing vivaria for garter, ribbon and water snakes: a large water bowl or permanent fixture containing water; an area on which to bask in light; a land area that is cooler than the rest of the cage; and shelters which can be used as hiding places.

Water container/section
Many people have successfully used medium to large dog water bowls for adult garter and ribbon snakes. However, for most water snakes, a larger container should be used. A polystyrene storage box is an effective water container and can be easily cleaned and

disinfected. It can be partially buried in the substrate of a naturalistic vivarium and still be removed for cleaning, with little effect on the whole. To prevent spillage, the lid can be left on the container and a large hole cut in the lid to allow for easy access. In order to prevent water spillage once a snake is immersed, all water containers should be no more than half-filled. For those who wish to integrate the water area into the overall design, a piece of glass or plexiglass can be affixed in such a way as to partition off a section of an all-glass vivarium. This can be accomplished by cutting the glass to the proper size and gluing it into the enclosure with a clear silicone sealant. This should be thoroughly cured and tested for leaks <u>before</u> the rest of the vivarium is assembled. One problem with fixed water areas is that water replacement is difficult and time consuming. A system allowing for easy drainage (such as a drain hole, with a hose and shut-off valve), easy cleaning and disinfecting of these fixed water areas is highly recommended. <u>Never use your mouth to start a siphon</u> when changing the water in these fixed water sections. An invaluable tool for changing water in small water areas is a wet/dry-type vacuum cleaner.

Problems with moist substrates
When water is spilled onto the cage's substrate it can become soggy. If you live in an area where normal relative humidity is low, wet substrate will usually dry out in 24 hours, so there is little cause for concern. However, water condensation and spillage do cause problems in areas with high relative humidity. This is because the substrate remains wet for long periods; in fact, in very high relative humidity areas, such as Florida, it may never dry. This wet substrate will lead to skin infections in these species within a very short period of time. Although the author recommends large water containers, especially for highly aquatic species (see Species Accounts), one simple solution to prevent wet substrate is to provide small water containers; the snake can't get into the container and therefore can't spill water. Providing enclosures with good ventilation will prevent excessive condensation.

Basking branch or wood section
Since most *Thamnophis* and *Nerodia* species are fond of basking in the sun on branches and other structures overhanging the water, a branch, section of cork bark, tree stump and/or section of root can be included in your design. This wood section should be at least as thick as the body of your snake and should be secured in such a way that it will not move. An unsecured branch could fall and cause serious harm to the snake.

Shelter

A shelter or hiding area will be essential for the well being of your snake. There are several options currently available in pet stores or specialized reptile stores. A piece of cork bark is an attractive and durable hiding area. If it becomes dirty simply wash it and it's as good as new. There are also different brands of pre-formed plastic or contrete shelters available that will work well. If rocks are stacked on top of each other to create shelters, they should be fastened together with silicone sealer or hot glue to reduce the possibility of an animal being accidentally crushed. Do not place shelters beneath a basking light unless you also place an extra shelter in the cool section of the vivarium.

Plants

Plants can easily be kept with garter snakes and water snakes. The most recommended method is to place plants growing hydroponically in jars of water inside the vivarium. Pothos *(Epipremnum aureum)*, arrowhead plants *(Nephytis)*, Chinese evergreen *(Aglaonema commutatum* and *A.* "Silver Queen"), monstera and silver wandering Jew *(Zebrina pendula)* are hardy and attractive choices for garter snake and water snake vivaria. The jars containing plants can be concealed behind wood or rock to give a more natural impression. Plants can also be introduced in pots. A wide variety of tropical plants that can grow in shade or partial shade will fare well with these snakes. In naturalistic vivaria, plants can be grown directly in the growing medium. Once again, it is important to remember that the substrate surface <u>must</u> remain dry, something which is easily accomplished by adding a layer of orchid bark to the surface. The author does not recommend the use of plastic plants with snakes or any amphibian or reptile. Why create ugly, artificial looking environments, when combining natural elements to make aesthetically pleasing vivaria is so simple? The key to keeping live plants growing will be the right type of lighting. A fluorescent fixture, running the length of the vivarium with two full-spectrum bulbs, such as Vita Lite®, will be ideal. Do not add so many plants that monitoring the snakes you are keeping becomes difficult. Prune the plants regularly when they become overgrown.

Heating & Lighting

Thermoregulation

All snakes are dependent upon their environment to regulate their body temperature. In other words, they cannot produce their own body heat. The popular term for this is "cold-blooded," but "ectothermic" is the correct term used by herpetologists to describe such animals. It means having a self-regulated (regulated by moving from place to place) body temperature, dependent upon environmental heat sources. Actually, cold-blooded is a misnomer; a snake that has been basking in the sun can have a body temperature that exceeds the ambient air temperature at that moment.

What are the consequences of being dependent upon the environment for temperature regulation? First, since snakes don't need to eat in order to provide body heat, they don't have to eat as often as mammals do. Indeed, many adult snakes rarely eat more than once a week and some may eat as seldom as once a month (the latter is not true for natricine snakes). To compliment this, a snake has a relatively slow metabolism, which means it digests its food much slower than a bird or mammal. Also, if a snake becomes too warm, it simply moves to a cooler spot, like the shade of a tree or underground burrow. Because most *Thamnophis* and *Nerodia* species are relatively small and have a high surface-to-volume ratio, they tend to heat up and cool down relatively quickly, which necessitates more movement in order to regulate body temperature within their optimum range. At night, the more temperate species tend to become inactive, while species found in Florida and on the Gulf Coast are often found to be active at night during warmer months of the year.

Several of the snakes discussed in this book are from a temperate climate and therefore (in the wild) must deal with winter temperatures that could result in torpor and/or eventual death. Most people believe that during cold weather snakes enter a mode of inactivity called hibernation. However, researchers in the field of herpetology consider hibernation to be exclusive to mammals and certain other forms of vertebrates, and not applicable to reptiles. Indeed, during the cold weather months most reptiles remain somewhat active and might even take advantage of an unusual warm spell to emerge from their dens and bask. This type of overwintering is termed "brumation" by herpetologists.

Do *Thamnophis* and *Nerodia* species in captivity need to be cooled in order to simulate seasonal changes? The answer is yes and no. Species from the northern United States and Canada, such as the Canadian red-sided garter snake, should be hibernated (brumated). First, because many will go off feed by the time winter comes along and they will lose less weight if they are not hibernated; second, because hibernation is part of their normal biological cycle. Keeping snakes at normal maintenance temperatures when they are off feed will usually result in drastic weight loss, which in turn may compromise their health. Snakes from warmer climates (such as the southern United States) which are kept as pets don't need hibernation, but may slow their food intake or even go off feed for a short period during the winter months. For those of you who plan to breed your snakes, research has shown that seasonal cooling plays a critical role for breeding success, not only in triggering breeding behavior, but also in stimulating higher rates of fertility. Having a suitable cooling facility for your snakes should be a major factor in deciding to breed or not to breed your snakes.

The need for vivarium heat gradients
Garter, ribbon, and water snakes should be provided a temperature gradient within the cage. This gradient will allow them to thermoregulate as necessary, seeking higher temperatures after feeding or when gravid, and cooler temperatures when at rest. These snakes should be maintained at a temperature range of 72 to 84°F (22.2 to 28.9°C) during the day, with a nighttime range of 68 to 74°F (20 to 23.3°C). In addition, many of the species discussed in this book enjoy basking in the sun at various times during the day. Thus, it will be essential to provide a basking area (the high heat component of the temperature gradient) in the cage; the basking area temperature should not exceed 88°F (31.1°C).

Basking
Among many snake breeders little emphasis has been placed on light; many snake species are kept and bred in dimly lit or dark enclosures heated by rheostat-controlled heat cables. However, if you have had the opportunity to observe some of the natricine species, particularly water snakes of the genus *Nerodia*, you will have noticed that many species bask in sunlight. While living in Florida, the author was able to observe this behavior on numerous occasions, particularly with green water snakes and red-bellied water snakes, but also with banded water snakes and even mangrove water snakes. The fact is that many natricines do bask. Basking allows these partially aquatic species not only a thorough

drying of the skin, but also an exposure to natural sunlight that may help kill or prevent the growth of certain bacteria and fungi. Until one sets up a large vivarium with basking sites, one will often not notice the importance of this behavior in these snakes. Thus, the author recommends (at least with water snakes) that large enclosures be provided; enclosures that allow for the design of basking sites with spotlights and full-spectrum lighting.

Creating basking sites
Incandescent bulbs
The easiest way to create a basking site while also providing light is to use an incandescent bulb in a reflector-type fixture. A vivarium at least 24 in. long will allow enough space for the use of this form of heating. Smaller enclosures do not allow enough space for creating a temperature gradient, which will result in a serious risk of overheating. The reflector and bulb should be placed <u>above</u> the screen at one end of the vivarium. Thus, one end of the vivarium will be warm while the other will be cooler, allowing a snake to choose the temperature gradient it feels is best for thermoregulating from moment to moment.

Infrared ceramic-element bulbs can be used as an alternative heat source to create a basking site in larger vivaria (at least 24 in. L x 18 in. H), when combined with fluorescent full-spectrum lighting. Like regular incandescent bulbs or spotlights, these can be connected to a rheostat in order to control the temperature. With smaller vivaria, a small subtank heat pad will be a better and safer heat source than an incandescent bulb in a reflector-type fixture.

Heat pads
Subtank heat pads are an alternative to incandescent bulbs in reflectors. These pads should be small enough that they cover only one end or one side of a vivarium. There are now several brands on the market. FlexWatt®, Tropic Zone® and Ultratherm® (which also sells thermostats) are some of the popular brands. Tetra Terrafauna® and ZooMed® also manufacture reptile heat pads. These subtank heating units should be controlled by rheostat or thermostat.

Hot Rocks
Pet stores have been selling "hot rocks" for years as a means of providing a warm basking area inside the tank. Unfortunately, early models maintained surface temperatures that were too high, causing thermal burns on the skin of whatever reptiles spent too much time on them. Recent hot-rock models have lower surface

temperatures and some even come with built-in thermostats. They are useful if one cannot, for whatever reason, provide better heating systems, such as the basking-light/subtank-heater combination mentioned above. The use of any hot-rock-type heater should be strictly monitored, using a reliable thermometer to verify a surface temperature not exceeding 88°F (31.1°C).

Thermometers

When using a heating system, whether incandescent bulb, heat pad or heat cable, a thermometer should be used to measure the temperature at the basking (warmest) site. The temperature should not exceed 88°F (31.1°C) in the area closest to the heat source. There are now many thermometers available in the trade. The least expensive type is the high range strip-type thermometer that can be adhered to the side of an enclosure. Glass-enclosed thermometers will also work well. The best type of thermometer is the digital electronic type with remote temperature probe. The probe is placed wherever the temperature needs to be determined while the electronic readout is in your hand. These can be purchased at electronic supply stores, such as Radio Shack.

Temperature controls

There are now several thermostats which are useful in herpetoculture. The most widely used device for controlling heating elements (e.g., heat pads, heat cables) is the light dimmer switch, which is essentially a rheostat. The rheostat-controlled heat is adjusted using a thermometer and some experimentation is needed to come within acceptable temperature parameters. Caution: Light dimmers are very limited in application due to their low voltage capacity; exceeding their capacity may result in an electrical fire.

A much more sophisticated thermostat developed specifically for herpetoculture is the pulse-proportional type. These thermostats have a temperature knob which is controlled via a remote sensor placed inside the area being heated. The thermostat feeds a steady, low-voltage pulse of electricity to the heating element, which will gradually heat up or cool down, dependent on the temperature setting. This type of thermostat is ideal when they work. The author has had more than one of these break down at very inconvenient times. Hopefully, reliability will increase in the near future. There are now at least three brands of pulse-proportional thermostats on the market. Check reptile magazines for sources if you cannot find them in your area. There is also a programmable day/night thermostat now available from Custom Reptile Network®.

Additional lighting
Full-spectrum lighting
For those wishing to have a well-planted vivarium, the use of full-spectrum fluorescent lighting, such as Vita-Lite® (Duro Test), is essential. This type of light also has the advantage of giving your snake some ultraviolet light, which may be beneficial for overall health.

UV-generating lights
Short exposures of 30 minutes to 3 hours per day to UV-A-generating bulbs, such as BL blacklights, or to the new UV-generating reptile bulbs expected to appear on the market in the near future, may be beneficial for basking species of natricine snakes.

This setup is similar to that on page 14. A water section has been added to the vivarium in place of a large bowl. Plants are grown directly in the substrate. Illustration by Margaret Hawley.

Ventilation

For vivaria that are all glass with full screen tops, air exchange will not be a problem. However, for wood or plastic enclosures, some consideration must be given to proper ventilation. The use of wire mesh screen material must be incorporated into the design of the wood cage so that air can flow from one side to the other, and preferably through the top as well. This is particularly important with this group of snakes, because the large water containers will combine with heat to result in a high level of water evaporation. The water vapor without good ventilation will end up condensing on the sides of the enclosure, creating a damp situation that will be detrimental to one's snake(s). With plastic storage boxes, sections of the lids or sides can be cut out and replaced with screen material. It is <u>very</u> important to thoroughly secure the screen to prevent escapes. An alternative to screening plastic cages is to drill several small holes in the sides and lids.

Cleaning & Hygiene

Cleanliness is extremely important for the long-term health of your snake. The water container must be cleaned and disinfected whenever there is <u>any</u> fecal matter or food in the water. A cat litter scoop can be used for any material that needs to be removed from the floor of the cage. If vivarium components become soiled, they too must be removed and cleaned. A 5% solution of household bleach in water is an effective disinfectant, as long as it is followed by a thorough rinse.

Even though *Thamnophis* and *Nerodia* love the water, this does <u>not</u> mean their substrate material can be wet or damp. In nature, the soil surface tends to dry quickly following exposure to the sun. Most natricines, even if they occur near water, will tend to alternate between the water's edge and dry areas such as overhanging branches or ground surfaces that are relatively dry. A damp substrate should be avoided; it will provide conditions that can lead to serious skin infections. Thus, any damp/soggy substrate should be replaced. One way to avoid a damp substrate is to make certain your snake cannot spill water out of the container, either by overfilling or tipping. A quick visual check every day will indicate what, if any, cleaning needs to be performed.

Feeding

How Snakes Eat

All snakes are carnivorous. *Thamnophis, Nerodia, Natrix* and *Amphisema* are fond of fish, frogs, newts and earthworms (to name a few) in the wild. It is probably due to this varied diet that these genera are found in such a wide variety of habitats. Garter, ribbon and water snakes should be considered opportunistic feeders, and thus offered as varied a diet as possible.

Snakes usually feed on large prey items which they swallow whole. This has led to certain physical adaptations, especially of the skull. Most of the bones of the head are held together by flexible joints allowing independent movement of each side of the upper jaw and the lower jaw. This results in phenomenal distortion, allowing the swallowing of truly large prey. To prevent prey from escaping, the teeth are sharp and pointed slightly back toward the throat. Because snakes' ribs attach only along the spine, the other ends (with flexible tips) are unfixed and able to separate; also, the skin stretches to allow passage of food through the digestive system.

Garter, ribbon and water snakes rely on eyesight (visual stimulus) and smell (olfactory stimulus) to detect prey. They are attracted to certain types of small animal movements, especially if reinforced by a stimulating scent (such as *Eau de Fish* or *Parfum de Frog*). The olfactory aspect of prey recognition is what leads many of these snakes to feed on dead prey, such as roadkill. They will also feed on mice that have been scented with fish or tadpoles. Once aware of a potential prey, these snakes move with exceptional speed to capture it. Following capture, a prey item is eaten quickly, shoved in by alternating motions of the snake's jaws, often while the prey is still alive. Unlike constricting snakes, garter snakes and water snakes subdue their prey by sheer jaw power, and suffocation of the prey usually results after it has entered the digestive tract.

These snakes are not necessarily discriminating in terms of potential prey. The author has found Florida garter snakes on the road, desperately trying to eat road-killed frogs and toads that were flat as pancakes. This carrion-eating behavior has been documented by other authors, but should never be a part of your snake's diet!

Food Items

In the wild, garter, ribbon and water snakes eat fish, frogs, tadpoles, newts, earthworms and even insects. In captivity, providing this variety of diet can be impractical. The following are guidelines for feeding these species of snakes; also, types of food that provide

The first step in fish filet preparation is to cut the filet in strips about 2/3 the width and 2-3 times the length of the head of the snake(s) to be fed.

Next, a vitamin/mineral supplement mixture is combined in a jar. In this case, 1 part Rep-Cal® vitamin D3/calcium supplement, 1 part Rep-Cal® Herptivite and 1/2 part brewer's yeast (B vitamin source).

Using a spoon, the mix is sprinkled lightly on the strips which are also rolled into any mix which may have fallen onto the cutting board.

adequate nutrition, are readily available, and relatively inexpensive. Note: these species feed on a wide variety of prey in the wild and will need some variety in captivity in order to remain healthy.

Fish filet, easily found in any major supermarket, can make up a significant part of the diet of these snakes. The filet should be from a high-quality, non-oily fish. Commercially raised catfish work well and can be frozen and used as needed. Be sure the pieces are completely thawed but not cooked. Soaking in a closed plastic bag placed in warm water is an effective way to thaw the filet.

> To avoid thiamin deficiency (see dietary disorders), fish filet sections should be heated to 180°F for five minutes and then cooled before serving. The defrost function of a microwave oven is ideal for this purpose.

If you have access to one of the huge discount warehouses that sells food, you may be able to find inexpensive fish filet sold frozen and in bulk. The author has found snapper filet sold this way at $2.00 per pound. Because fish filet has no bones, skin, or other fish parts which might provide essential dietary elements, a vitamin/mineral supplement must be added to the fish to avoid the possibility of dietary deficiencies. The author recommends a mix consisting of 50% reptile multivitamin/mineral powder and 50% calcium/vitamin D3 powder, such as Rep Cal®. A light sprinkling of the mix on one side of fish filet sections once or twice a week will be adequate.

The fish should be thawed and cut into pieces that are approximately 1/2 the width of the head and 1 to 1 1/2 times the length of the head of the snake. Place the pieces on a small dish and sprinkle them with the vitamin/mineral supplement. Place the dish in close proximity to the water container or offer the fish sections with the use of forceps. Try feeding 2 or 3 pieces for the first few times fish is given. You will need to experiment to know how many pieces to feed at one time. Fish filet can make up 1/2 to 2/3 of the diet. Although individuals have been successful with supplemented fish filet as an exclusive diet, the author recommends that whole fish or scented mice be offered every 2 to 3 feedings.

Feeder goldfish and/or guppies of appropriate size will provide variety to the diet and will be eaten with relish by all of these species. Guppies are ideal for initial feeding of newborns and hatchling natricines. Feeder fish can be placed in the water container or in a shallow bowl of water near the main water container. With reluctant feeders, placing live goldfish on the floor of the

enclosure and allowing them to flip about will often elicit reluctant feeders to grasp prey. Another alternative is to place the fish in a bowl with only a small amount of water, once again causing them to move and break the surface. If fish are placed in water that is too deep or a container that is too large, the snakes, particularly garter snakes may have difficulty catching them. Feeder goldfish and guppies are readily available at any pet store, but they can be expensive as a primary diet if your snake refuses fish filet. Inexpensive alternatives are smelts and small bait fish found at bait and tackle shops. Bait fish that have been seined or netted from the wild have the potential of introducing parasites to your snake. The risk of parasites is reduced by using commercially raised bait fish.

Earthworms can be fed to provide some variety in the diet of natricines. The worms can be purchased at bait shops and some pet stores. Offer common earthworms rather than nightcrawlers; avoid redworms, which are particularly foul tasting to these snakes. If you want to collect your own worms, care should be taken to avoid areas where garden chemicals may have been used. Whether bought or collected, the worms should be rinsed to remove dirt and put into a shallow bowl. The worms can be chopped up for hatchlings and ribbon snakes. Earthworms should be used as a supplement to the main diet. They can be important for getting recently acquired wild-caught snakes to begin feeding. Caution: earthworms have the potential to pass intestinal parasites to your snake.

Frogs and tadpoles comprise a significant part of the diet for these species in the wild. Sometimes they can be purchased in bait shops or you can expend the time and energy to collect them yourself. If you are willing to set up an aquarium, then tadpoles can be raised, fed flaked tropical fish food, and fed off when needed. Once again, caution is advised because frogs and tadpoles have the potential to infect your snake with internal parasites and bacterial diseases.

<

Top left: Garter snake is attracted by motion and smell of live goldfish in a shallow container.

Top right: It enters water and attempts sideswipes at fish.

Middle left: A fish is caught.

Middle right: Using alternating left and right jaw movements, it positions and directs the goldfish toward the mouth/throat area.

Lower left: The upward movement of the right side of the jaw is clearly visible during the last stages of ingestion.

Lower right: The fish, now in the esophagus, can be swallowed. Note the bulging neck area.

Commercially raised rodents will sometimes be accepted by some of these species, especially larger garter snakes found in the western United States. The most common approach to induce your snake to eat a rodent is a method called scenting. Essentially a pre-killed mouse (body girth equal to or less than thickest girth of the snake) is thoroughly washed with mild, unscented soap and water, thoroughly rinsed, and rubbed on a piece of raw fish (with several *Thamnophis* species, earthworm slime also works). The mouse can then be fed directly to the snake by holding it with forceps, or it can be placed on a dish as you would when feeding pieces of fish. You can also place the scented mouse on a dish containing another piece of fish. Once your snake has begun to feed on mice, it can usually be switched to frozen mice obtained from most pet stores. To avoid problems, thaw the mouse completely. This can be accomplished by placing it in closed plastic bag in bowl of warm water.

Commercial prepared diets for garter snakes and water snakes are now available in Great Britain and should eventually become available in the United States. There are probably opportunities for individuals interested in developing new products in the form of prepared natricine snake diets.

Forceps feeding
Forceps can be purchased from medical supply companies or specialized reptile dealers. Offering food items from forceps allows one to carefully monitor how much a snake eats. It also

Forceps feeding a section of supplemented fish filet to an Eastern garter snake.

allows one to simulate movement in dead animals or fish filet sections. Forceps will prove a handy tool for anyone keeping these snakes. They will allow for the individual feeding of snakes and are quite useful when keeping snakes in groups.

Feeding Schedules for Hatchlings and Subadults

Hatchlings will usually start feeding within days after their first shed (7-10 days after hatching). Feed both hatchlings and sub-adults every 3-4 days. Both of these age groups will stuff themselves if overfed. You should strive for a steady, controlled growth rate; thus, give them adequate food, but don't give them so much that there is an unnatural bulge in their midsection.

Feeding schedule for adults

Adult garter and ribbon snakes can be fed on a once-per-week schedule. In general, water snakes tend to have a slightly faster metabolism and thus need to be fed every 5 days. For adult females that are going to be bred and those already gravid, the feeding schedule should be accelerated to every 4 to 5 days in garter and ribbon snakes, and every 3 to 4 days for water snakes. Serve several frequent small meals, especially when the gravid female is close to the time of giving birth. The advantage of frequent smaller-than-normal meals is that they tend to keep a gravid female on feed up to the time of birth, instead of her going off feed 1 to 2 weeks before giving birth. This will allow the female to retain a reasonable amount of weight, and may enable her to produce a second clutch.

Dietary Disorders

Captive snakes which are fed only frozen fish and are not supplemented with vitamin/mineral powder will develop a vitamin B1 (thiamin) deficiency. This can result in a nervous system disorder with symptoms of lack of muscle control. Fish contains an enzyme which breaks down the thiamin before it can be digested by the snake. To avoid this, heat the fish to 180°F (80°C) for five minutes to destroy the enzyme. Be certain that the vitamin/mineral supplement used contains vitamin B1. If your supplement has no vitamin B1, it can be purchased in powdered form at the local health food store and added at a rate of 8 to 10 mg per 1 lb of supplement.

Another common dietary problem is called steatitis, which is basically a vitamin E deficiency. It results in large fat deposits under the skin. This typically occurs as a result of feeding a snake a diet of oily fish containing large amounts of unsaturated fats. A varied diet, along with the use of less oily fish, will certainly help to prevent this problem.

Handling

As a general rule, some wild-caught garter, ribbon and water snakes exhibit certain behaviors which are not conducive to handling. Garter snakes and ribbon snakes tend to emit a foul-smelling material produced by their musk glands, while water snakes will also attempt to bite. However, with a minimum of effort many of these snakes will eventually calm down and allow themselves to be handled. **Caution:** Rear-fanged Asian water snakes are occasionally imported and sold in the pet trade. These can inflict a venomous bite, so be certain of the identification of any snake you have purchased, particularly Asian water snakes. Also, there are very rare reports of someone having an allergic reaction to the saliva of a garter snake after having been bitten. Depending upon the degree of the reaction, a doctor may have to be consulted.

Handling procedures

One way to approach handling a snake is to begin touching it while it is inside its cage. The animal gradually becomes accustomed to human touch. If the animal attempts to bite, the use of a leather gardening glove is recommended. Some of the natricines, particularly large water snakes have a bite that can be quite painful; bleeding and in some cases even scarring can result. If the snake musks, the use of latex gloves, such as used for washing dishes, will keep the smell off your hands. The next step is to pick up the animal. Again, the use of gloves during initial handling attempts is recomended, particularly with water snakes. Once in hand, utilize minimal restriction rather than firm restraint, essentially guiding the snake as it moves through your hands. Restraint will be interpreted by a snake as a definite threat; this will often result in a quick turnaround and biting. Eventually, after several attempts at handling, your snake should become comfortable being touched and should stop biting. However, there are certain species and certain individual snakes that will resist any attempt at taming and regular handling; these animals should be considered strictly as display animals. One problem with many of the natricines is that because they live near water or sometimes in branches overhanging water, they do not have the hesitation that some of the constricitng snakes have about falling off someone into midair. Handling these snakes over a table should give somewhat greater control. Always wash your hands with a bacteriocidal soap, such as Betadine® scrub, after handling these snakes. This is especially important for children and the elderly. It is recommended that immuno-compromised individuals not handle reptiles of any kind.

Butler's garter snake *(Thamnophis butleri)* becomes available in good numbers during late spring. Being a northern species, hibernation is essential for their long-term maintenance. Photo by James Gerholdt.

The Eastern blackneck garter snake *(Thamnophis cyrtopsis ocellatus)* has an extremely limited range in Texas. They can be observed hunting around cattle tanks and ponds during the day. Photo by Brian Hubbs.

The Santa Cruz aquatic garter snake *(Thamnophis couchi atratus)* is found from San Francisco Bay south to Monterey. Photo by Brian Hubbs.

Giant garter snakes *(Thamnophis couchi gigas)* are the largest of all garter snakes, reaching a maximum length of 58 in. (1.45 m). This specimen has an unusually bright mid-dorsal stripe. Photo by Brian Hubbs.

Wandering garter snakes *(Thamnophis elegans vagrans)* will travel several miles from the nearest body of water. They adapt well to captivity and can easily be switched to fish-scented rodents as a main source of food. Photo by Bill Love.

An amelanistic albino wandering garter snake *(Thamnophis elegans vagrans)*. This particular specimen happened to be gravid when collected by the author. Photo by Philippe deVosjoli.

The checkered garter snake *(Thamnophis marcianus)* is one of the more attractive garter snake species. Photo by Bill Love.

An albino checkered garter snake *(Thamnophis marcianus)* collected in Texas. Albinos of this species are the most readily available albino morphs of the genus. Photo by James Gerholdt.

A Northwestern garter snake *(Thamnophis ordinoides)* from Washington state. Photo by James Gerholdt.

The Gulf Coast ribbon snake *(Thamnophis proximus orarius)* is characterized by its broad gold vertebral stripe. Photo by Brian Hubbs.

A Peninsula ribbon snake *(Thamnophis sauritus sackenii)* eating a small Cuban tree frog *(Osteopilus septentrionalis).* Photo by Bill Love.

This Plains garter snake *(Thamnophis radix)* is just beginning its shed. Failure to provide adequate humidity can result in shedding problems. Photo by James Gerholdt.

An adult Plains garter snake *(Thamnophis radix)* eating its preferred prey, an American toad *(Bufo americanus)*. Photo by James Gerholdt.

A species with very limited distribution, the narrow-headed garter snake *(Thamnophis rufipunctatus)* is found in mountainous areas of Arizona, New Mexico and old Mexico. Photo by Brian Hubbs..

A red-spotted common garter snake *(Thamnophis sirtalis concinnus)* from near Portland, Oregon. Photo by Bill Love.

A common garter snake *(Thamnophis sirtalis)* from Minnesota. Members of the *sirtalis* complex tend to be docile. Photo by James Gerholdt.

An amelanistic albino red-sided common garter snake *(Thamnophis sirtalis parietalis)*. Photo by James Gerholdt.

The "red phase" of the San Francisco garter snake *(Thamnophis sirtalis tetrataenia)*, one of the most beautiful natricines. An endangered species, the U.S. Fish and Wildlife discourages captive-breeding because they claim it would become difficult to distinguish captive-bred specimens of this easily bred snake from illegally collected wild specimens. Although captive-bred animals are occasionally available in Europe, this subspecies is not available in the United States. Photo by Brian Hubbs.

A melanistic phase of the mangrove water snake *(Nerodia clarkii compressicauda)*. This is one of the most sought after of the North American water snakes, although it tends to be more difficult to establish than other species. Photo by Bill Love.

A red phase of the mangrove water snake *(Nerodia clarkii compressicauda)*. Although found near brackish waters, this species should be kept like other water snakes. Selective breeding for red and orange specimens should eventually result in some spectacular morphs. Photo by James Gerholdt.

A Florida green water snake *(Nerodia floridana)*. These snakes, when encountered in the wild, are large, impressive and nasty. Captive-raised specimens tend to become tame. They require large enclosures and large amounts of fish to fare well. Photo by Bill Love.

A red-bellied water snake *(Nerodia e. erythrogaster)*. This attractive species is reported to travel short distances from bodies of water, but the author has only observed them coiled on branches overhanging water. Like many water snakes, their disposition leaves much to be desired, but many specimens do eventually become tame. Photo by Bill Love.

A blotched water snake *(Nerodia erythrogaster transversa)* from Betar County, Texas. Photo by Bill Love.

The author's amelanistic Florida water snake *(Nerodia fasciata pictiventris)* is the focus of a selective breeding program. Photo by Philippe deVosjoli.

The Florida water snake *(Nerodia fasciata pictiventris)*. This species is commonly available in the pet trade. Photo by Bill Love.

The diamondback water snake *(Nerodia rhombifera)* is one of the most attractive species and is also easy to keep. Usually, it will readily switch to a scented-rodent diet. Photo by James Gerholdt.

An albino diamondback water snake *(Nerodia rhombifera)* from Biloxi, Mississippi. The attractive appearance of albino and other odd morphs of water snakes has played an important role in increased herpetocultural interest in this genus. Photo by James Gerholdt.

A Midland water snake *(Nerodia sipedon pleuralis)*. Photo by Bill Love.

The scaleless morph of the Northern water snake *(Nerodia s. sipedon)* is seldom available in herpetoculture. This is a healthy, viable specimen which, when handled, feels like soft, smooth rubber. Photo by James Gerholdt.

Albino Northern water snakes *(Nerodia s. sipedon)*. Photo by James Gerholdt.

Unlike the adults, babies of the brown water snake *(Nerodia taxispilota)* adapt well to captivity. Captive-raised specimens are quite attractive, with rich browns and well-defined patterns. Photo by Bill Love.

Children should be instructed to never put their hands in their mouths or rub their eyes while handling these snakes. Do not allow these snakes free run of the house, i.e., do not allow them to crawl across kitchen tables, sinks and/or counters. Do not use sinks and bathtubs used by humans when cleaning cages, etc. Practices such as these can spread diseases.

Daily Quick-Check of Snakes & Cages

Routine visual inspection of your snake and its cage on a daily basis should be the foundation of your husbandry technique. The following inspections should be performed daily to prevent serious diseases and accidents.

1. **Muscle tone/vigor:** Does the snake move in an easy manner or does it move only when prodded? Are there any perceived depressions or bumps on the body? When the snake is picked up, does it feel strong in your hands?

2. **Weight assessment:** Do the ribs or backbone show through the skin, even though the snake feeds well?

3. **Eyes and mouth:** Do the eyes appear alert and clear, without being sunken in? Are there any lumps, bumps, or bruises on or around the mouth?

4. **Vent and fecal assessment:** Is the vent area clean and free of any caked or runny fecal matter? Do the feces appear firm, with normal color, or are they watery, off-color, or terribly smelly?

5. **Behavior:** Is the snake gaping its mouth? Does it appear to have an equilibrium loss, to be listless, or ceaselessly move about the cage?

6. **Cage assessment:** Make sure the substrate material is clean and dry, cage furniture is secure, and water and water bowls are clean. Any shed skin should be removed, along with any fecal matter.

If problems are seen during steps 1-5 above, a visit to the veterinarian is recommended. At the very least, a fecal analysis should be performed by a veterinarian.

Diseases & Disorders

Parasites

There are two general classes of parasites commonly found: internal parasites and external parasites. For the most part, external parasites, which include ticks and snake mites, are rarely found on *Thamnophis* and *Nerodia* species. This is probably due to their frequent immersion in water. On the other hand, internal parasites are commonly found in these genera, the most common being amoebas and flagellate protozoans,

External Parasites

Ticks: Visual inspection will reveal small gray or brown bumps on the surface of the snake's skin if it has ticks. The tick imbeds its mouth parts in the skin between the scales. There are several ways of removing ticks. A pyrethrin spray, available from veterinarians, is quite effective. Simply spray a cotton swab, apply the medication to the tick, wait a few minutes and remove the tick with tweezers. If the tick is imbedded near the snake's head, pyrethrin is not recommended. In this case, with a cotton swab apply a drop or two of rubbing alcohol or a small amount of petroleum jelly directly on the tick. Wait 5 to 10 minutes and remove the tick with tweezers. Whenever pyrethrins are used, be sure to <u>thoroughly</u> rinse the snake in lukewarm water after treatment is completed.

Mites: These are seen as tiny, dark, bead-like creatures crawling on the skin of the snake. A good indicator of mites is the presence of tiny white specks on the skin. These are mite feces and, in severe cases, look like white dust on the snake's skin. Pyrethrin spray is very effective in killing adult mites, as well as their eggs, which are also laid on the snake's skin. The best method of applying pyrethrin is to dampen a cloth with the spray and wipe the snake with the cloth. Make sure all of the skin is covered, including the top of the head and the chin and throat area. The eyes <u>must</u> be avoided as pyrethrin can damage the lens of the eye. Cages and cage furniture can also be treated with pyrethrin spray. Everything must be rinsed thoroughly before being used again. A 5% solution of chlorine bleach in water, followed by a thorough rinse, is also effective for killing mites in cages and on furniture.

Internal Parasites

Probable signs of internal parasites include: lack of appetite, weight loss, little or no growth, runny stools, regurgitation and dehydration. A snake with these symptoms must be treated or it will die.

For positive identification of parasites, a fresh stool sample should be taken to the nearest reptile veterinarian. The veterinarian will analyze the sample or it will be sent to a laboratory for analysis. This procedure is relatively inexpensive.

Protozoans and amoebas inhabit the lower intestinal tract of snakes. The drug of choice to eliminate these parasites is Flagyl® (metronidazole), administered orally. It can be obtained in powdered form from most pet stores, where it is sold to treat protozoan diseases of tropical fish. The dosage to use is 10 to 25 mg/lb. (25 to 50 mg/kg); repeat in 3 or 4 days. If the snake is still eating, instead of dipping the preferred food in powdered vitamins, dip it in the measured dose of metronidazole. If the snake refuses food, then the drug must be introduced by a tube inserted down its throat. A veterinarian should perform this procedure.

Trematodes, or flukes, are very common internal parasites in all reptiles whose diet includes fish and amphibians, food items acting as intermediate hosts for flukes. Garter snakes and water snakes can ingest them with their food. Sometimes flukes can be observed in the mouth and throat area, although they don't typically manifest symptoms requiring veterinary help. However, if trematode ova are discovered in a stool check, it is highly recommended that you treat with Praziquantel (Droncit®-Mobay) at 8 mg/kg administered orally and repeated at the same dosage 2 weeks later.

Other common internal parasites are nematodes, which also inhabit the gastrointestinal tract. Use oral treatment, with Panacur® (fenbendazole) at a dosage of 10 mg/lb. (25 mg/kg); repeat in 2 weeks. At least 3 treatments are necessary to eliminate nematodes. Fenbendazole paste can be obtained at feed stores and large discount pet stores that handle horse care products.

Skin Disorders
Garter, ribbon and water snakes are very susceptible to skin blister disease. This bacterial infection occurs when the substrate within the cage becomes damp and stays damp day after day. The blisters appear as white bumps all over the skin. The substrate should be changed to a dry one immediately. If it is a mild case, once dry substrate is provided the snake's skin should heal with the next shed. In more severe cases, washing the skin with Betadine® solution once per day until the condition clears may be necessary.

Mouthrot (Infectious stomatitis)
Mouthrot is a disease which affects the tissue of the gums. Symptoms vary with the severity of the infection. Swelling along the

jawline causes the labial scales to protrude in a way that is not normal. Examine the inside of the mouth along the jawline. To do this, firmly but gently hold the snake just behind the head so that it cannot move; with the other hand, pull down on the lower lip to expose the jawline. If stomatitis is present, there may be an accumulation of caseous (cheesy-looking) matter. Most cases of stomatitis can easily be treated at home. The mild initial stages of stomatitis can be treated topically. The caseous matter should be removed using cotton swabs soaked in a 3% hydrogen peroxide solution. By gently holding the snake behind the head, the swab can be pushed against the gums. After removing the caseous matter, irrigate along the jawline with a mouthwash solution (3 parts lukewarm water to one part mouthwash). Betadine® or Viadent® mouthwash solution should be applied to the affected area at least once a day. A small spray bottle can be used to administer the Betadine® or mouthwash solution. With conscientious treatment, this disease should clear up in two to three weeks.

Stomatitis is <u>very</u> infectious and can be transmitted to other snakes. Please disinfect hands and any tools used after <u>each</u> treatment.

Respiratory Infections
Respiratory infections can occur in captive garter and water snakes when they are kept at temperatures too cool for normal thermoregulation or at temperatures that are too warm during hibernation. Early symptoms include the presence of bubbly mucus in the mouth, listlessness, and decreased appetite. If left untreated, the amount of mucus increases and the snake keeps its mouth open and its head partially raised. Ultimately, untreated respiratory disease leads to the death of the snake.

In the early stages of respiratory infection, raising the cage temperature to 86 to 89°F (30 to 31.7°C) around the clock will enable the snake's immune system to fight any infection. More advanced symptoms will require veterinary help and the use of injectable antibiotics. After one week of increased cage temperature, if there is no improvement in your snake's health, a veterinarian should be consulted.

Gastrointestinal Infections
Typical symptoms of gastrointestinal disorders may include: repeated regurgitation of food; loose, smelly, or discolored stools; loss of appetite; dehydration; weight loss; and listlessness. Any snake with these symptoms should be taken to a veterinarian to determine the cause and to provide effective treatment. Untreated

snakes with these symptoms usually die, but with proper diagnosis and treatment the snake has an excellent chance of surviving long-term.

Two recent articles (spring 1993) appearing in very popular herpetocultural publications addressed the issue of *Salmonella* bacteria in reptiles. The basic conclusion from each article was that the debate still continues about whether these bacteria are always present and whether they normally manifest clinical symptoms or not. The agreed-upon points were that *Salmonella* <u>can</u> be transmitted to humans by reptiles, and that treatment of reptiles with bactericidal agents is largely ineffective. Recommendations included strict quarantine of reptiles found to harbor *Salmonella* plus strict personal hygiene by anyone handling the animals or cage furnishings.

If your snake exhibits any of the symptoms above, strict quarantine and maintenance procedures should commence <u>immediately</u>. The affected snakes should be taken to a veterinarian, along with a fecal sample. Personal hygiene is critical during the quarantine period. Disinfectant <u>must</u> be used to wash hands and any tools used for snake maintenance. Quarantined snakes should be maintained only <u>after</u> regular maintenance of your established collection. Following work with sick animals, <u>never</u> handle healthy animals.

Baby garter snakes or water snakes that refuse to feed can be hand fed guppies: the edge of the mouth is slightly opened, a pre-killed guppy gently inserted, head first.

Breeding

General Information

Garter, ribbon and water snakes usually breed between March and June in the wild, depending upon the latitude of their area of origin. Northern species tend to breed later than southern species, probably because they are subjected to longer periods of cooling (and lower temperatures) during the winter.

The time between copulation and birth for garter, ribbon and water snakes is approximately 12 weeks, but it is temperature dependent. For some species of *Nerodia* and *Thamnophis* from south Florida, this period can be only 7 or 8 weeks, while in Canadian species it might be as long as 5 months.

It is well documented and worth noting that female garter snakes have the ability to retain sperm from a previous year's mating. So if you have a female garter snake that gave birth last year but doesn't have access to a male this year, don't despair. Although there is usually a significant drop in fertility, it is still possible that she might give birth to babies this year. Garter, ribbon and water snakes are born in a clear membranous sac which breaks open when it touches the ground.

Some species of garter snakes, such as the popular and beautiful red-sided garter snakes, spend the winter months in large groups in communal dens. The males are reported to become active sooner than females, waiting outside the den for females to emerge. It has been suggested that for consistent breeding results with garter snakes, particularly with species that form congregations, several males be available to one female. However, good breeding results have been reported by herpetoculturists with single pairs of adult snakes.

Pre-breeding Considerations

1. **Size/age:** Adult size can be determined by checking the species accounts in this book. Undersized females which are bred tend to have difficulty giving birth and then never reach full adult size. With most species, these snakes should be at least 18 months old (second year following birth) before breeding is attempted, although under optimal rearing conditions some species will be sexually mature by one year.

2. **Sexual pairs:** Visual identification of male and female *Thamnophis* and *Nerodia* species is mostly dependent on the degree of post-cloacal tapering of the tail. Males tend to have a longer, more

gradual taper, while females have a shorter tail with far greater tapering, no doubt related to the absence of hemipenes. If positive visual sexual identification cannot be made, then a sexing probe may be employed by someone experienced in its use. This thin, blunt-tipped instrument is inserted into one of two openings in the sides of the cloaca and penetration depth is measured by counting scales. In general, females will probe to a depth of 3 or 4 subcaudal scales while males will probe as deep as 8 to 10 scales.

3. **Health/weight:** Snakes which are being considered for breeding should appear to be in perfect health. The animals should possess good weight (a rounded appearance with no ribs or backbone visible) and there should be no signs of respiratory or skin infections. If there are any doubts about their health status, then do not consider them for breeding.

Newborn checkered garter snakes *(Thamnophis marcianus)* in a basic shoebox setup with paper towel substrate, shelter and water container.

Pre-Breeding Conditioning

Although the *Thamnophis* and *Nerodia* species that have been described inhabit diverse habitats, general parameters have been established that will result in breeding success with these species. These parameters includes a period of reduced temperature and photoperiod, followed by an accelerated feeding schedule when the snakes are first placed back in normal conditions.

Little research has been done on biological activity during the winter months when reptiles are subjected to cooler temperatures. Most herpetologists seem to assume that snakes simply hibernate, just as certain mammals do. However, the little research that has been completed suggests that reptiles do not "shut down" for the winter, but have the capacity to emerge from their dens, if possible, when there is a stretch of warm weather. In effect, reptiles seem to be more in a state of biological waiting than in a state of extremely slowed metabolic rate. This is most likely accomplished by having winter dens which are well below the freeze line of the ground. At a depth of 18 to 24 in. below the ground surface, the temperature will remain at a constant which is well above freezing.

This leads us to a definition of the wintertime metabolic state in reptiles: "brumation." Brumation should be considered the form of hibernation applicable to reptiles. However, for the sake of simplicity, "hibernation" will be used for the period of cooling necessary to breed most *Thamnophis* and *Nerodia* species.

Hibernation is necessary for more consistent breeding results. The period of cooling is reported to stimulate the production of hormones in both males and females. When the snakes are returned to normal temperature and light conditions, these hormones stimulate reproductive behavior, the production of pheromones in females, and the production of active, healthy sperm in males. Ovulation by females usually occurs after they have been bred. The eggs are fertilized by stored sperm.

For those who plan to hibernate snakes, a simple strategy should be followed. Most herpetoculturists plan to start cooling their snakes in November or December, depending upon when their locale cools down to the desired temperature. (Hibernation for most species normally ends sometime in March.) Many herpetoculturists accelerate the feeding schedule for their snakes 6 to 8 weeks before hibernation. This builds up body fat reserves needed for sustaining good body weight during hibernation. Before snakes enter hibernation, a fasting period of 10 to 14 days is necessary to rid the digestive tract of food and fecal matter. Since hibernation involves a considerable reduction in metabolic rate, the chance of a bacterial "bloom" within the gut of a snake is increased if food is still present. Feeding is discontinued throughout the hibernation period, although fresh water must be provided at <u>all</u> times.

Hibernation Methods

Hibernation involves cooling the snakes for a specific period of time and at a specific, consistent, lowered temperature range. Most of the species of *Thamnophis* and *Nerodia* should be placed in an area with a constant ambient air temperature of 50 to 60°F (10 to 16°C). The area should be quiet and dimly lit. Some breeders provide artificial light, but for a reduced period of time (9-10 hrs/day). Other breeders have had success hibernating their animals in dark areas during the entire time. If room temperature is too warm but outside nighttime temperature is cool and there is a window in the room, it can be opened at night and closed during the day. The use of a window fan will help bring the cool air into the room. The area where hibernation takes place should be monitored with a thermometer for a week prior to introducing snake cages. Ideal thermometers are the digital electronic type that can give high and low temperature readings within a 24-hour period. If the hibernation area is too cool, set up heat tapes wired to a thermostat. This is much safer and more reliable than using an electric space heater.

Most of these snake species can tolerate temperatures as low as the 40's°F (4.4 to 9.4°C) for short periods of time. Certain species which inhabit the most southerly ranges of garter and water snakes undergo very little cooling in the wild. The mangrove water snake (*N. clarkii compressicauda*), Florida green (*N. floridana*) and Florida water snake (*N. fasciata pictiventris*), which can be found in extreme southern Florida, have been bred using no cooling period. The Florida garter snake (*T. sirtalis similis*) can be included in this group. If little or no breeding success occurs, then a hibernation period of 6 to 8 weeks at 60 to 65°F (16 to 18°C) should be tried.

It is important to check hibernating animals periodically for any type of problems, especially respiratory disorders. If there is a problem, the snake should be removed from hibernation immediately and provided with appropriate medical treatment.

If your snakes are healthy coming out of hibernation, they can be returned to normal maintenance temperatures and given extended daylight hours (i.e., 14 hrs. of light). They should be offered food within 2 or 3 days after the start of normal temperatures, but might require as much as 7 to 10 days before they begin to feed. Live goldfish are a good way to start them feeding again. Once started, the schedule for feeding should be every 3 to 4 days. This schedule should continue until the female goes off feed just before giving birth or laying eggs, in the case of the oriental striped garter snake.

Pairs can be kept together after being removed from hibernation or they can be kept separately, if you have the room and are willing to do the maintenance on more than one cage. If they are kept separately, introduce the male into the female's cage following their first shed after coming out of hibernation. This usually corresponds to the females' pre-ovulating/pheromone-producing period and is very critical for successful breeding.

After successful breeding is observed, the accelerated feeding schedule should continue, especially for the female. If the male is separated from the female, he can be put on a normal feeding schedule of every 5 to 7 days.

Cage furnishings for gravid females should include their normal water container with fresh water plus a nest box where the babies can be born. For live-bearing snakes, damp straw mixed with vermiculite is a good medium inside the nest box. For egg-laying natricines, moistened vermiculite will provide the proper medium for depositing eggs. Once the eggs are laid, the box can be removed from the cage, the eggs buried 2/3 into the vermiculite and incubated at 82 to 84°F (27.8 to 28.9°C).

A good nest box is a plastic storage box with the lid on and a small hole cut in the side, through which the snake can enter and exit. If subtank heating is provided, then the box can be placed in a warm area. With oriental garter snakes, if eggs are being incubated the entry hole should be sealed and a few smaller holes made in the lid to allow for air exchange.

Baby garter snakes will readily feed on guppies.

Rearing Babies

Garter snakes and water snakes can be very prolific, especially many of the *Nerodia* species. For optimal control and growth, it is recommended that babies be segregated, either singly or in groups of 3 or 4 babies. To accomplish this, space- and labor-effective systems need to be devised. One system consists of housing individual babies in gallon jars or small plastic terraria. The lids of the jars should be perforated with several small holes for ventilation. Another approach is to cut out a section of lid and glue a section of screening over the opening, using either silicone sealant or hot glue. Commercial plastic terraria have narrow slits in the lids that allow for plenty of ventilation; at the same time, they are narrow enough to prevent the escape of most natricine babies. Another popular method to house these baby snakes is plastic storage boxes. By adding a small shelter and a water dish, one of these boxes will readily accomodate a group of babies. Remember: Perforate the lid and sides with fine holes to provide ventilation. Newspaper, high quality paper toweling and/or butcher paper make ideal ground media for these temporary containers. Babies usually start feeding after their first shed, which occurs 7 to 10 days after birth. A good choice for a first food is small guppies. Baby water snakes and garter snakes will get excited by both the smell and the motion of a guppy jumping about. Finely cut and supplemented pieces of fish filet can also be offered. Babies of many garter snake species are particularly drawn to small earthworms. These can be tried, although other foods are generally preferable. Look under rocks or fallen branches for "baby" earhtworms these snakes can consume. If a baby does not appear to be feeding, it should be isolated and worked with more closely. This might include offering food items most likely found in the wild, such as tadpoles and earthworms. The size of the food items should be such that they are easily swallowed by a baby snake. Since baby *Thamnophis* and *Nerodia* are not born with a significant amount of egg yolk reserve, they must be offered food soon after their first shed.

If a baby natricine refuses food time after time, force feeding might be the only way of keeping the animal alive until it begins to feed on its own. A small pre-killed feeder guppy will be easily force-fed if inserted head first into a baby snake's mouth. Often a baby snake will finish swallowing the guppy on its own once it has been partially introduced. An alternative used by some herpetoculturists is to use a section of mouse tail from a prekilled adult mouse. This can be inserted, thick end first into the snake's mouth using forceps. As soon as the food has been introduced into the snake's mouth, put the snake gently back into the cage and do not disturb it for half an hour. You can then check to see if the snake swallowed the food or regurgiated it. If the snake did not appear to be very stressed from the force feeding, then this procedure can be repeated on a normal schedule until it is feeding on its own.

Another example of a basic setup for garter and ribbon snakes. Orchid bark is used as a substrate and barely damp moss is used for shelter. An incandescent bulb in a fixture is used to provide heat. Note the strip thermometer to monitor temperature.

Notes on Select Species

Because the great majority of garter snakes and water snakes sold in the pet trade are wild-collected, it is important to properly identify the species you have bought or collected. This information is sometimes critically important and could mean the difference between success and failure in keeping and breeding. The following are descriptions and information regarding the distribution and behavior of the most commonly found *Thamnophis* (garter and ribbon snakes) and *Nerodia* (water snakes) species. Albino strains of several species have been established in herpetoculture. The large scale which covers the cloaca of these snakes is either single for garter snakes and ribbon snakes or split in two for American water snakes. All of the *Thamnophis* and *Nerodia* species bear live young.

Butler's garter snake *(Thamnophis butleri)*

Butler's garter snake is found in southwestern Ontario, Canada, eastern Michigan, eastern Indiana, and western Ohio. It inhabits lowlands, wet meadows, swamps, and lake shores, but will also occur in drier open areas. It spends most of its time under logs, tree stumps, and in thick grasses; it can be found in the morning and at dusk, as it leaves its hiding place in search of food or to warm itself.

It reaches a maximum length of 27 in. (68.6 cm), although most specimens are 15 to 20 in. (38.1 to 50.8 cm). The head is long and somewhat narrow, with almost no differentiation between it and the neck area. There are three stripes running the length of the body; one down the back which is whitish-yellow, and one along each side which is either yellow or orange. The background color of the back is brownish-black with light brown between the side stripes and the belly. Depending on how dark the background color is, black spots or blotches can be seen between the stripes. The belly is usually grayish-green and mottled. An albino strain has been established.

This small species can be kept successfully in a modest-size vivarium, equivalent to a 10 gallon aquarium. Half of the enclosure space should be devoted to water, with a shelter such as cork bark provided for this relatively shy species. Despite its shy nature, it will usually allow gentle handling without musking. This species must be hibernated 4 to 5 months during the winter, with breeding taking place in April. Babies (up to 16 per litter) are small, so baby guppies and finely chopped earthworms are necessary to get them feeding.

Aquatic garter snake *(Thamnophis couchi)*

The aquatic garter snake, which includes 6 subspecies, is found from southwest Oregon south to Baja, California, and from coastal California to western Nevada. This species is the largest of the garter snakes, with *T. couchi gigas* (the Giant garter snake) reaching lengths of up to 4 ft. All of the subspecies are mainly aquatic and diurnal (active during the day). They can be found sunning on branches or on the banks of streams and ponds.

Depending on the subspecies, maximum length is anywhere from 18 to 57 in. (45.7cm to 1.45 m.). Coloration also varies quite a bit, depending on the subspecies. Over most of its range, however, the stripe on the back is faint or is just a series of blotches, with only the coastal California subspecies showing any real definition. The stripes on the sides are also faint or blotched. The Sierra garter snake (*T.c. couchi*) has a dull yellow background color, which is checkered with dark brown blotches. Side stripes are very faint and the back stripe is narrow and dark, and fades toward the tail. The Coast or aquatic garter snake (*T.c. aquaticus*) has a yellow to orange stripe running down the back with the side stripes being more subtle in color. The background color is dark olive to black, the throat is yellow and the belly is dark yellow or pale red. The Santa Cruz garter snake (*T.c. atratus*) resembles the aquatic garter snake except that the side stripes are fainter. Sometimes there are dark spots between the back and side stripes, and it has a bluish belly. The giant garter snake (*T.c. gigas*) is the largest of all garter snakes, reaching lengths of over four feet. The background color is olive-brown, with spots arranged in a checkered fashion down the back. It has a faint, narrow stripe on the back and sides. The two-striped garter snake (*T.c. hammondi*) has almost no sign of a stripe on the back, but does have yellow stripes running along the sides of the body. The background color is olive, gray or brown, with dark spots on the sides between the stripes and the belly. The Oregon garter snake (*T.c. hydrophilis*) has a faint yellow stripe down the back, with the side stripes being even fainter or completely lacking. The background color is gray, with poorly defined but conspicuous dark spots arranged in a checkered pattern. The belly is a light color with no markings.

Black-neck garter snake *(Thamnophis cyrtopsis)*
Depending on which reference is consulted, there are from 3 to 6 subspecies. In any case, this species is found in southeastern Utah, southern Colorado, eastern Arizona, New Mexico, and south into Mexico, Belize, and Honduras. The differences of opinion as to the number of subspecies center around whether *T. cyrtopsis* has integrated with the Mexican garter snake, *T. eques*, or whether they evolved separately. These snakes are usually found near water, including streams, springs, and cattle tanks, although they will wander into the desert during summer rainstorms. They occur from low elevation Sonoran and Chihuahuan desert to pine-covered mountainsides and meadows. This species is diurnal and can be found during the day, hunting or basking on rocks or on stream banks.

The head of this species is bluish-gray to black on top and is easily identified by the neck area. It derives its name from two large black blotches just behind the head, separated by the beginning of the orange stripe running along the middle of the back. There are side stripes which are less distinct and vary in color from light gray to yellow. Large black or blue-black spots are found between the back and side stripes. Maximum length is a little over three feet.

This is a moderately large garter snake that is mild mannered and adapts well to captivity. A vivarium the size of a <u>long</u> 20 gallon aquarium can house an adult pair. The water area can be 1/4 to 1/3 of the floor space. Pieces of fish filet, and scented pre-killed pink and/or fuzzy mice will be readily eaten. Hibernation is a must for 3 to 4 months at 50 to 60°F (10 to 15.6°C).

Western terrestrial garter snake *(Thamnophils elegans)*

There are 4 or 5 subspecies of this garter snake, depending upon which reference is consulted. *Thamnophis elegans* is distributed over a wide area ranging from southwestern Canada to Baja, California, east to South Dakota and south to northern Mexico. They occur in a wide variety of habitats, from grassland at sea level to mountain meadows at 9,000 feet. They are found in close proximity to water. The diet of *T. elegans* is quite varied, which allows for easy adaptation to a captive environment. These are diurnal snakes that can be seen hunting or basking during the day. Large numbers of *T. elegans* have been found to spend the winter months together in communal dens.

Maximum length is a little over 3 feet. Basic body color is brown with a whitish-yellow stripe down the back and less distinct stripes on the sides. The area between the back and side stripes is either black or has dark spots or light specks. The Mountain terrestrial garter snake (*T.e. elegans*) has very distinct back and side stripes; the back stripe is light orange; the belly, light gray with no pattern. The Klamath terrestrial garter snake (*T.e. biscutatus*) varies from *T.e. elegans* in that the stripe on the back is bright yellow; the belly, dark gray. The wandering terrestrial garter snake (*T.e. vagrans*) has a dull yellow or brown stripe on the back, fading toward the tail. The side stripes are also barely defined, with dark spots between them and the back stripe. The top of the head is light brown; the belly, light gray. The Coastal terrestrial garter snake (*T.e. terrestris*) has a well-defined yellow stripe down the back, but varies from other subspecies with similar stripes in that it has light red to orange dots on the sides and the belly.

Adults of this species can be kept singly in 10 gallon vivaria or large sweater boxes. Adult pairs should be kept in 20 gallon vivaria. The water area can be 1/4 or less of total ground area. A very adaptable species, it will normally eat any of the food items discussed here, including mice. However, the author's female amelanistic albino wandering garter snake refuses anything but live feeder fish. Hibernation should be 4 to 5 months in the low 50's°F (10 to 15°C) for successful breeding. Expect 10 to 15 babies which will eat small feeder guppies immediately and readily switch to fish filet. This species has a reputation for eating its young, in addition to any other small snake it might happen to find. Prompt removal of newborns is <u>highly</u> recommended. Caution: Be aware that the female, if not in the breeding mode, and pestered by a male, will sometimes kill him.

Checkered garter snake *(Thamnophis marcianus)*

This attractive species ranges from east Texas and central Kansas, west to southeastern California, and south to the northern half of Old Mexico. Even though they are found in arid and semi-arid regions, they are almost always close to water. As more and more arid and semi-arid land is converted to irrigated farms, the range of checkered garters seems to be expanding.

The chief distinguishing marking of this species is the dark checkerboard pattern down the back on a brownish-yellow ground color. There is usually a pale yellow stripe running down the middle of the back. This pattern is very attractive and has helped make it one of the most popular garter snakes. The albino form is by far the most widely available, having been bred in good numbers for several years; the checkerboard pattern is comprised of red squares on an off-white background.

One of the more heavily-bodied of the garter snakes, checkered garter snakes range in size from 18 to 42 in. (45.7 to 106.7 cm), with 24 to 30 in. (61 to 76.2 cm) being average. A single adult can be housed in a 10 gallon vivarium (20 in. L (50.8 cm)) with pairs in 29 gallon vivaria (30 in. L (76.2 cm)). The water container can be 1/6 to 1/4 of the total ground area. This species is normally very gentle and wild-caught adults tame quickly. They will readily eat fish filet, earthworms, live feeder fish and scented small mice. Hibernate for 3 to 4 months during the winter; breeding will take place from late April through May. Expect from 10 to 20 babies which are very hardy and adapt quickly to captivity.

Plains garter snake *(Thamnophis radix)*

The Plains garter snake has two subspecies which occur from south-central Canada south to Colorado, Kansas and western Missouri. They are found in areas near water, such as stream banks, ponds, irrigation ditches and swamps, and inhabit lowland prairies, farmlands and mountain meadows. Maximum length is 40 in. (101.6 cm), with typical lengths from 20 to 28 in. (50.8 to 71.1 cm). This is also a diurnal species and can be seen hunting or basking during the day.

The stripe on the back is usually bright yellow but it can be orange. The side stripes are less bright and are greenish or bluish to pale gray. There are rows of black spots between the back and side stripes, as well as rows of black spots running down the body below the side stripes. Background color varies from gray to reddish-brown. The two subspecies look very much alike, the main difference being the number of scale rows on the neck and the number of scales on the belly. This species can be kept in a manner similar to *T. elegans*.

Common garter snake *(Thamnophis sirtalis)*

Here again, the number of subspecies represented is disputed among zoologists. With 12 or 13 subspecies, *T. sirtalis* is the most common, widely distributed, physically variable snake of the genus. Some subspecies are rarely available and are not discussed here.

Thamnophis sirtalis is found all across the southern part of Canada and in all lower 48 states in the United States, except Arizona and New Mexico. All of the subspecies in this group prefer a watery habitat and thus can be found in just about every conceivable habitat associated with water. However, they have been found in fields and woodlands, as well. They are primarily diurnal, but it appears the warmer climate subspecies become active in the evening at certain times of the year. Several albino strains exist in herpetoculture. Depending upon size and subspecies, *Thamnophis sirtalis* will give birth to 14 to 20 young.

Eastern common garter snake: *T.s. sirtalis* has yellow stripes on the back and sides with a background color of black, brown, green or olive. It usually has a row of prominent black spots running between the stripes that often overruns the side stripes. The belly is pale gray, becoming darker toward the tail, and has dark spots as well. It is a diurnal snake and has been found to move only short distances within its territory. Maximum length is 48 in. (1.22 m.), with most specimens 18 to 26 in. (45.7 to 66 cm). *Thamnophis s. sirtalis* is probably the most popular garter snake in the pet trade due to its availability.

Red-sided common garter snake: *T.s. parietalis* has broad, dull stripes on the sides, and a well-defined stripe on the back. It has red bars running between the stripes; the top of the head is mostly olive and the belly is green or yellow with dark spots.

Florida garter snake: *T.s. similis*, also referred to as the blue-striped garter snake because side stripes are bright blue. The back stripe is dull tan to yellow; background color, brown to dark brown. Maximum length is 39 in. (99.1 cm), with typical size 20 to 26 in. (50.8 to 71.1 cm). Captive-bred albino specimens have recently become available.

San Francisco garter snake: *T.s. tetrataenia*, considered not only the most beautiful garter snake, but one of the most beautiful snakes in North America. A wide greenish-yellow back stripe that is edged with black is then followed by a red stripe on either side, then a black stripe on either side of that. The top of the head is red; the belly is greenish-blue. Considered an endangered species, its range is restricted to San Mateo County, California. It is included in this book because of its beauty; also because some zoos have them on display.

Western ribbon snake *(Thamnophis proximus)*
The Western ribbon snake and the Eastern ribbon snake (*T. sauritus*), are distinguished from garter snakes mainly by the extreme slenderness of their bodies, longer tails (25 to 33% of total body length) and the complete absence of markings on the belly. *Thamnophis proximus* ranges from southern Wisconsin to the Gulf Coast, south as far as Costa Rica, west to New Mexico and east to the Mississippi Valley.

The background color varies from olive-brown to black, with the back and side stripes a well defined light yellow to orange. Maximum length is 37 in. (94 cm), with normal length from 20 to 30 in. (50.8 to 76.2 cm). The head is generally dark in color, with two lighter spots occurring side by side in the center toward the back of the head.

Considering its range, this is a highly adaptable species and should be viewed as semi-aquatic. It is found in a variety of habitats, from temperate grasslands to tropical swamps. It is diurnal in habit and can be seen hunting or basking on a branch or rock overhanging the water during the morning and late afternoon.

Eastern ribbon snake (Thamnophis sauritus)
The Eastern ribbon snake, as mentioned before, is very slender, the head is barely distinguished from the neck, and the eyes are large with round pupils. The back and side stripes are usually clearly defined and are yellowish-orange to dark tan; the body color varies from reddish-brown to dark brown. Maximum length is up to 38 in. (96.6 cm), with average lengths of 18 to 26 in. (45.7 to 66 cm).

Thamnophis sauritus ranges from Michigan south to Mississippi, east to Florida and north to the southern half of New England. It is semi-aquatic and always found near the edges of bodies of water or swamps and streams. This species is diurnal and likes to sun itself on trees or other vegetation that has fallen in the water. As with all other *Thamnophis* species, it will swim away when disturbed.

The cage requirements should include a water area which is at least 1/3 of the total floor space. A branch or two for basking and a shelter are highly recommended. It is usually hit or miss in terms of adapting this species' eating habits to fish filet. In many cases they refuse to eat anything but live feeder fish or tadpoles. There is very little interest in breeding this species, but 3 to 4 months of hibernation should be sufficient conditioning. Up to 20 young per litter.

American water snakes: Genus Nerodia
This is a group of harmless, semi-aquatic snakes often seen basking in the sun on logs, branches, floating vegetation or any structure allowing quick access to the water. They are excellent swimmers and will dive when alarmed, which is usually not the case with garter snakes. Most of their diet is obtained in or near the water.

Water snakes regularly get themselves into trouble with humans, through no fault of their own, by having an appearance similar to the cottonmouth (*Agkistrodon piscivorus*), which is a venomous snake. Most people don't look closely enough to determine the snake to be harmless and thus in fear thoughtlessly destroy it.

Most water snakes will flatten their body when threatened and if picked up will release large quantities of foul smelling musk from glands at the base of the tail; they will also strike and bite very hard.

Since these water snakes are commonly available and the European ones (*Natrix*) are not, only American species will be discussed in this book. However, most of the husbandry techniques that will be presented here are also suitable for European species. American water snakes range throughout the eastern half of the U.S. and into northern Mexico. Florida, Mississippi, Louisiana, and Texas are the states which have the greatest numbers of *Nerodia* species.

Salt Marsh snake *(Nerodia clarkii)*

There are three subspecies, *N.c. clarkii*, *N.c. compressicauda* and *N.c. taeniata* (which is protected). The popular mangrove water snake *(N.c. compressicauda)* is not usually available in any quantity (wild-caught or captive-bred), but it is of some interest to the author. Termed mangrove water snake because it inhabits the mangrove swamps of South Florida's east and west coasts, it is a comparatively small water snake; its maximum size is 36 in. (91.4 cm). Colors and patterns are variable: black, dull yellow or greenish, usually with dark spots or crossbars. There is a very attractive red or orange-red color morph with no crossbars. The tail is supposed to be slightly compressed, although the author has never encountered this.

The mangrove water snake can be observed basking in the sun on the tangled roots of mangrove trees. It usually hunts at night. It mostly inhabits bodies of water that are salt or brackish and is only occasionally found in fresh water. This snake has not adapted to drinking salt water, so it must obtain metabolic fluids through the ingestion of its prey. In captivity, they will drink fresh water only over time, gradually becoming accustomed to having it available. Fresh water must be provided at all times.

The mangrove water snake breeds from mid-to-late March. If sexual pairs of this subspecies (*compressicauda*) are not together by early-to-mid March, chances of successful copulation are diminished. This snake has been bred with no formal hibernation technique. However, to ensure good fertility, hibernation for 6 to 8 weeks at 60°F (15.6°C) is recommended. Young orange or red phase specimens of this water snake are among the most beautiful of the natricine snakes.

Green water snake *(Nerodia cyclopion* and *floridana)*

Green water snakes range throughout the southeastern United States, being found in Florida, Georgia, South Carolina, Alabama, Mississippi, Louisiana, Texas and Arkansas. These species can be said to prefer slower, quieter waters that include reeds and water lilies to bask on, along with overhanging branches. *Nerodia cyclopion* and *floridana* can be active day or night. This is evidenced by finding them lying on asphalt roads after sun has set; they can also be found hunting frogs that are active at night.

These two snakes differ from all other *Nerodia* in that they have a row of scales between the eyes and an upper row of scales along the lips (labial scales). The Florida green *(N. floridana)* can grow to 74 in. (1.9 m.) in length, with 30 to 55 in. (76.2 sm to 1.4 m.) the normal range; the green *(N. cyclopion)* watersnake's maximum is 50 in. (1.3 m.), with 30 to 45 in. (76.2 cm to 1.1 m.) being normal. The Florida green has an olive or brownish ground color on the back and sides with very little distinct pattern. The whitish-gray belly also has few or no markings. The ground color of the green water snake is also olive to brownish, but it does possess faint dark bands across the back and light spots or crescents on the brownish, whitish-gray, or yellowish belly.

Large specimens of green water snakes have proportions reminiscent of anacondas and make impressive displays. These species fare well in large vivaria (6 ft. L x 18 in. W) with large water containers. Expect newly acquired wild-caught specimens to bite, but with persistent handling some can become quite tame. These are very adaptable snakes and will eat fish filet or bait fish. Breeding occurs in April and these large natricines will give birth to a large number of offspring (up to 101 on record!). Hatchlings adapt well to captivity and will eat feeder guppies. Plan on 3 to 4 months of hibernation at 50 to 60°F (10 to 15.6°C) during the winter months as a prerequisite for breeding.

Plainbelly water snake *(Nerodia erythrogaster)*
This group includes four subspecies, with the following being the most easily obtainable: *N.e. erythrogaster*, the redbelly water snake (also known as the "copperbelly"); *N.e. flavigaster*, the yellowbelly water snake; and *N.e. transversa*, the blotched water snake. The Northern copperbelly, *N.e. neglecta*, rounds out this group.

Nerodia erythrogaster ranges from southern Delaware to north Florida and west through Alabama, Mississippi, Louisiana and Texas. It is typical of other water snakes in terms of its aquatic nature, inhabiting the well-known swamps of the Southeast, as well as canals, irrigation ditches and lakes. It is quick and agile in the water and will not hesitate to bite first and then musk, if necessary. In hot, humid weather this snake is known to travel large distances from its home waters.

Nerodia e. erythrogaster is reddish-brown to chocolate brown on the back and sides. The belly, for which it is named, is red to reddish-orange without any markings. Only the young of this subspecies have markings on the belly.

Nerodia e. flavigaster is gray or grayish-green on the back, usually without pattern, sometimes with light bands across the back. The belly is yellow and often has an orange tint with no other markings found.

Nerodia e. transversa has wide, dark brown bars down the back on a background of gray or brown and rows of dark blotches down the sides. The belly is light yellow with an orange tint.

This species fares well in captivity in larger vivaria containing a large water area and branches for basking. They will adapt to eating fish filet. Even though wild-caught specimens bite vigorously, they will become tame with regular handling. This species must be hibernated 4 to 5 months for consistent breeding results. Breeding takes place in May and in early fall 20 to 25 babies are born. The babies are easy to raise and adapt quickly to eating fish filet.

Southern water snake *(Nerodia fasciata)*

Three subspecies comprise this group; *N.f. fasciata, N.f. pictiventris* and N.f. *confluens* are all commonly found in the pet trade. *Nerodia fasciata* ranges into North and South Carolina, Georgia, Florida, west to Texas and north to Missouri. It inhabits places where water is found and will even live near brackish swamps along the Gulf Coast. An excellent swimmer and diver, it can be found under debris near bodies of water, such as fallen trees and discarded building materials. During the summer it is active day or night, hunting fish and frogs, salamanders and earthworms. *Nerodia fasciata* can grow as long as 63 in. (1.6 m.), with 24 to 42 in. (61 to 106.7 cm) being about normal.

Nerodia f. fasciata, or the banded water snake, has dark bands across the back and a dark stripe from the eye to the corner of the mouth. The body color can vary from gray to brown to reddish-brown. The belly has square spots toward the sides, which also vary in color from reddish-brown to blackish-brown. It is worth noting that older specimens of *N. fasciata* tend to become extremely dark, which makes identification difficult.

Nerodia f. pictiventris, the Florida water snake, also has dark crossbands on the back and a dark stripe behind the eye. There are dark spots on the side of the body, more or less between the bands. The belly is yellow with wavy red or black lines running across.

Nerodia f. confluens is the broadbanded water snake, which has few, though very wide crossbands on the back. These bands vary in color from black to reddish-brown, with yellow as the background. In some parts of its range, the red or yellow can predominate, making it an extremely attractive snake.

This species is probably the most aquatic of all *Nerodia*, therefore must have a majority of its vivarium devoted to water. They love basking on branches under a heat lamp. They are inconsistent in terms of temperament, with some individuals biting vigorously while others allow themselves to be handled immediately after capture. In general this species can be considered gentle. Most subspecies need 3 to 4 months of hibernation for good breeding results. The banded water snake has been bred successfully without formal hibernation, although the author recommends at least two months of hibernation at 60°F (15.6°C). Mating will take place in April and early May for most subspecies. Up to 57 young per litter.

Diamondback water snake *(Nerodia rhombifera)*

This is another large, semi-aquatic water snake that is fairly common in its range of the Mississippi River valley from southwest Indiana to Kansas to the Gulf of Mexico and west to Texas. It inhabits large bodies of water, as well as ditches and cattle tanks. It has been known to inhabit rivers and streams that are surrounded by very arid terrain. During the heat of the summer it becomes almost exclusively nocturnal and can be found under logs and other debris during the day. *Nerodia rombifera* will sun itself on branches and rocks at other times of the year and can climb quite well. There are 3 subspecies.

The maximum length for adults is 63 in. (1.6 m.), with 30 to 48 in. (76.2 cm to 1.22 m.) the normal size range. The back is light brown to dirty yellow with dark, vaguely diamond-shaped markings which extend onto the sides. The belly is yellow with dark spots or half moons. A unique characteristic of adult males of this species is the presence of wart-like bumps (papillae) on the underside of the chin.

This species usually does well in a large vivarium with 1/3 to 1/2 of the area devoted to water, plus a solid branch to allow for basking. Some keepers have difficulty getting this species to adapt to captivity; also, only long-term, persistent handling will tame most wild-caught specimens. Hibernation is highly recommended for 4 to 5 months with breeding occurring from late April through May. Be prepared for a large number of babies (50 or more) which usually take a little longer to convert from feeder fish to fish filet.

Northern water snake *(Nerodia sipedon)*
This snake ranges from southern Quebec, Canada, south through the Middle Atlantic states to North Carolina and west to Alabama and Mississippi. It prefers quiet, slow-moving water, but will adapt to swifter waters, if necessary.

Maximum size is 53 in. (1.35 m.), with 24 to 42 in. (61 to 106.7 cm) being normal. With its wide geographic distribution, color variations occur from area to area. In general, the most prominent markings are reddish-brown to black crossbands on the neck and upper back. There are alternating blotches on the side and back that give it a zigzag appearance. The background color varies from pale gray to dark brown and the belly has dark half moons.

At least 1/2 of the area of this species' vivarium should be water, with at least one basking site. Wild-caught specimens normally don't bite, but they will musk when handled. This behavior stops with routine, gentle handling. Wild-caught adults easily convert to eating fish filet; the babies are extremely hardy and will feed readily. Hibernation is a must, even for pet snakes, for 4 to 5 months.

Brown water snake *(Nerodia taxispilota)*
This is a relatively heavy-bodied water snake which can grow as large as 69 in. (1.75 m.), with average size being 30 to 60 in. (76.2 cm to 1.5 m.). Because of its large size, it is sometimes mistaken for the venomous cottonmouth (*Agkistrodon piscivorus*). It ranges from southern Virginia to southeast Alabama to the southern tip of Florida. *Nerodia taxispilota*, even though it is usually found on the coastal plain, restricts itself to clear, still, fresh water. It is diurnal and can be

found sunning itself on branches overhanging the water.

The brown water snake's head is clearly set off from the neck, another characteristic which misleads people into thinking it is venomous. The background color is brown to dark brown, with even darker large, squarish blotches running in a row down the back. There is a row of these blotches on either side which alternates with the middle row. The belly is yellow to brown, with clearly defined dark blotches.

This species can be kept in captivity in a manner similar to the southern water snake, *Nerodia fasciata*. This is the second largest and perhaps the most ill-tempered American water snake. Wild-caught animals of this species <u>almost</u> <u>always</u> bite; there has been very little success in taming them. The brown water snake is prolific and will give birth to up to 58 babies per litter. Babies easily adapt to captivity, although wild-caught adults tend to present difficulties in acclimating to captive conditions. To date, there has been little or no interest in breeding this species. This species has a tendency towards obesity, once it is feeding well. Be careful of the type and the quantity of fish you feed this snake.

Oriental Garter snakes (Genus *Amphisema)*

Although there are several species, the one most commonly found in the pet trade is *Amphisema stolata* or striped garter snake. It has a wide distribution, ranging from Afghanistan to Indochina and includes the southern coast of China. It is found in lowlands, as well as hills, and mountains up to 6,000 ft. elevation. This species does not appear to be nearly as dependent on bodies of water, being found in open forests and grasslands. This is not to say that it dislikes the water. It can be seen basking on branches or reeds overhanging the water and drops into the water for protection.

The Asian striped garter snake is known to be reluctant to bite, thus making it a good candidate as a pet. Unfortunately, many imported specimens are heavily parasitized and often diseased. A significant percentage of imports do not fare well in captivity.

Eggs are usually laid 8 to 12 weeks after copulation for the Oriental striped garter snake (*Amphisema stolata*) and babies hatch 6 to 10 weeks after being laid. Oriental striped garter snakes hatch by breaking through their eggs with a temporary egg tooth attached to their snout. Hatchlings grow very rapidly and can become sexually mature at 10 to 12 months of age.

References

Conant, R. 1991. A Field Guide to Reptiles and Amphibians of Eastern and Central North America. Houghton Mifflin Co., Boston.

Frye, F. 1991. Reptile Care Vols. 1 & 2. TFH Pub.

Grier, J.W., M.S. Bjerke and L.K. Nolan. "Snakes and the Salmonella Situation." Bulletin of CHS, 1993, 28(3):   53-58.

Mader, D.R. and K. DeRemer. "Salmonellosis in Reptiles." The Vivarium. 1993, 4(4): 12-13,22.

Mehrtens, J.M. 1987. Living Snakes of the World. Sterling Publishing Co., New York.

Rossi, J.F. 1992. Snakes of the U.S. and Canada, Vol. I. Krieger Publishing.

Shine, R. 1991. Australian Snakes, A Natural History. Cornell Univ. Press. Ithaca, N.Y.

Stebbins, R. 1966. A Field Guide to Western Reptiles and Amphibians.

Sweeney, R. 1992. Garter snakes. Blandford, London.

Trutnau, L. 1986. Nonvenomous Snakes. Barron's, Hauppauge, N.Y.

Zug, G.R. 1993. Herpetology: An Introductory Biology of Amphibians and Reptiles. Academic Press, Inc., San Diego, CA.